Hertfordshire
COUNTY COUNCIL
Community Information

Suffolk
21/11/02.
7/12

942.
3
LAN

Please renew/return this item by the last date shown.

So that your telephone call is charged at local rate,
please call the numbers as set out below:

	From Area codes 01923 or 020:	From the rest of Herts:
Renewals:	01923 471373	01438 737373
Enquiries:	01923 471333	01438 737333
Minicom:	01923 471599	01438 737599

L32 www.hertsdirect.org

D1492406

Lost Ships of
the West Country

LOST
SHIPS
of the
WEST
COUNTRY

A guide to forgotten craft
from Poole to Gloucester

Martin Langley
& Edwina Small

STANFORD MARITIME

Stanford Maritime Limited
Member Company of the George
Philip Group
27A Floral Street, London WC2E 9DP

© Martin Langley & Edwina Small 1988

British Library Cataloguing in Publication Data

Langley, Martin
    Lost ships of the West Country.
    1. South-west England. Coastal
    waters.
    Abandoned ships. Sites. Visitor's
    guides
    I. Title   II. Small, Edwina
    914.23′04858

ISBN 0-540-07431-4

Typeset and printed in Great Britain
by BAS Printers Limited,
Over Wallop, Hampshire

The production of this book has been due to the goodwill and cooperation of a great many people, principally those whose names are printed below. Only a fraction of our research has been carried on in libraries and record offices. Research into hulks and ship-remains (and to the best of our knowledge there is no other book on the subject) involves setting out to find people – the people who know.

Once a ship has been de-registered, she disappears from written records; and once the generation of those who knew her passed away, her hulk becomes anonymous unless she achieved some fame or notoriety which was recounted to the succeeding generation. Many smaller vessels elude even de-registration and their ultimate fate is the more difficult to discover. Some harbourmasters are well-informed on ship-remains within their area of jurisdiction, and know their identities and when they were laid up. But this is the exception rather than the rule, for it seems there has never been any obligation to keep a local register of abandoned vessels, and the modern harbourmasters have more than enough to do since small-yachting reached its present proportions.

But in the absence of records, one of the most rewarding facets of hulk-research is the necessity to meet and talk with both active and retired seafarers, shipowners, harbourmasters, customs officers, lifeboatmen, masters, mates and crewmen, coastguards and longshoremen. Without exception we have found them the most delightful and helpful folk one could wish to meet. They have made our research, protracted and unremitting though it has had to be, wholly a pleasure.

We are also indebted to several distinguished authors on maritime subjects for their kindly co-operation and advice; and to others whose hobby is ship-research and who have willingly shared their knowledge and delved into their records on our behalf.

The list that follows is not comprehensive but we have tried to make it as nearly so as possible.

PUBLIC BODIES AND COMPANIES
Bridgwater Central Library, Bristol Central Library, Bristol City Docks, Bristol City Museum, British Waterways Board, Gloucester, Brixham Maritime Museum, Cobb's Quay of Poole, Cornish Calcified Seaweed Ltd, Exmouth Central Library, Falmouth Harbour Commissioners, Falmouth Maritime Museum, Fowey Harbour Commissioners, Fowey Museum Trust, Gallery of Old Newquay, HM Customs Exeter, HM Customs Plymouth, HMS *Raleigh* Torpoint, Liverpool Central Library, Maritime Museum Exeter, National Maritime Museum, National Trust Cotehele, Naval Historical Branch MOD, Newlyn Harbour Commissioners, North Devon Museum Trust, Philip & Sons, Dartmouth, Plymouth Central Library, Poole Harbour Commissioners, Poole Maritime Museum, Queen's Harbourmaster, Plymouth, Southampton Central Library, SS *Great Britain* Trading Ltd., Taunton Local History Library, Topsham Branch Library, Torquay Central Library, Truro Harbour Office, United Society for the Propagation of the Gospel, World Ship Society.

INDIVIDUALS
George Andrews of Plymouth, Percy Andrews of Dittisham, DG Attwood of Loughboro', Berly Badger of Plymouth, Chips Barber of Exeter, Peter Baker of Kenton, Terry Belt of Winchester, Martin Benn of Exmouth, Norman Benny of Falmouth, Frank Berryman of Falmouth, Mike Bevan of Fowey, Jack Birch of Plymouth, Ralph Bird of Carnon Mine, John Blower of Torpoint, George Bond of Galmpton, Frank Booker of Plymouth, 'Dido' Bradford of Exmouth, Jim Broad of Torpoint, Arthur, Fred & Leslie Brown of Plymouth, KV Burns of Plymouth, Barrie Butcher of Plymouth, Stephen Carter of Douglas, I of Man, Ian Childs of Penzance, Charles Codner of Hartlepool, John Cotton of Plymouth, Ron Cowl of York, Des Cox of Appledore, Jack Crawford of Millbrook, Jack Crosley of Antony Passage, Sid Cutler of Falmouth, Wilf Dodds of Bridgwater, Fred Drew of Teignmouth, DG Eley of Cotehele, Gordon Ferryman of Highbridge, Joe Frude of Plymouth, Bill Garland of Falmouth, Cyril Gascoyne of Penzance, Arthur Glinn of Plymouth, AJ Greaves of Poole, M Gregson of Appledore, Geoffrey Hamer of London, Edward Hannaford of Salcombe, Jack Harris of Appledore, Ken Harris of Dartmouth, PM Herbert of Bude, Stan Hewell of Mylor, Peter Hockings of Exmouth, R Hodges of Port Navas, Henry Irving of Bristol, Bill Jackson of Plymouth, Deryk James of Herne Bay, Tom Jewell of Appledore, Bill Lindsey of Padstow, Keith Macarthur of Birkenhead, Tom Marshall of Millbrook, Ian Merry of Bere Alston, Graham Mobbs of Southampton, Bob Morley of Bristol, David Murch of Salcombe, Mark Myers of Morwenstow, WH Newman of Topsham, Harold Norton of Topsham, Jim Norton of Topsham, GA Northey of Newquay, Mrs G Parish of Dunball, RM Parsons of Bristol, Bette Prosser of Plymouth, TW Prosser of Saltash, Florence Prout of Abbotskerswell, Bill Ricketts of Topsham, Adam Ridges of Poole, Fred Rowbotham of Stonehouse, John Scott of Bampton, Tony Skillman of Oxford, Tom and William Slade of Appledore, Billy Stevenson of Penzance, AV Stone of Watchet, Guy Sydenham of Poole, Alice Talling of Lanteglos by Fowey, Alan Tarr of Ramsey I of Man, R Thomas of Glasgow, John Tilling of Warrington, WJ Trebilcock of Truro, RD Turner of Poole, George Vallance of Kingsteignton, JF Voysey of Topsham, Ned Widger of Brixham, Len Williams of Padstow, Tom Williams of Dartmouth, Fred Wills of Poole.

Contents

Foreword

The commercial sailing ship and the steamship which ousted her have alike become memories for many of us. The authors are among those who regret their passing, while others might call it progress. Motor vessels also feature in these pages, but it is the ships of sail and steam, with the men who built, manned, or served them, that have largely created the maritime story of the West Country seaboard and the port of Plymouth. This book uncovers a little of that period which lies just around the corner in man's memory, so it is written for the nostalgic cruising yachtsman, the ship-lover and the local historian.

It is also, in a humble way, a book of marine archaeology. Whilst recording those few old vessels which have been preserved, or restored, or at least are still afloat, it mainly deals with the many whose remains lie in creeks or estuaries and have long been derelict. Some are no more than skeletons, perhaps only keel, bilge timbers and sternpost; others are dismasted hulls; yet all still betray the individual styles, peculiar skills or special techniques of their builders.

But it is hoped this book may also appeal to the holidaymaker who is minded to park his car and walk – or clamber – in lonely places. It lends point and interest to a walk to have a particular site to find, and a sense of adventure to reach a spot not easy of access: and when the derelict is found comes the exercise of imagination, reading her story and seeing her as once she was, afloat and earning her living.

Finally, there is something here for those who like nothing better than to 'mess about in boats'; for a number of the hulks are best approached by water. But here a word of warning will not come amiss: never approach a stranded hulk once the tide has started to ebb. Six hours marooned on a mudbank can seem like six days, and if your boat has been hired, such a miscalculation will prove expensive!

It is our hope that the use of this book will bring as much pleasure to the reader as its research gave to the authors.

This book is a joint effort throughout, but the first person singular always refers to Martin Langley.

Martin Langley
Edwina Small

Introduction

Wherever an arm of the sea reaches far inland and the salt water laps upon the sheltered dry earth of the countryside, here, in the area of drying mud which is neither properly part of the water, nor of the land, there arises a certain smell. It is the smell of brackish water, the last overflow of the sea, and of the weed and jetsam which finds its way to even so far an anchorage, and lies there about the tideline, alternately wetted by the rising water of the creek and dried by the sun and air, rotting until it becomes part of the mud.

Here, in this quiet half-sea world, the schooners passed their old age. For of all those ships which ceased to sail in the years between the wars more than half were abandoned, their owners dead or untraceable, to lie slowly falling to pieces in the quiet backwaters of Devon rivers and the remote creeks of Cornish and Irish roadsteads. Here they lay, between steep wooded hills, rising and falling twice each day. They were more than half their years aground, their masts leaning as they lay on their bilge strakes in the tidal ooze. At first seaworthy ships, often with the canvas still bent on their booms and yards, they slowly became more and more dilapidated. The men of the creekside villages stripped them of all movable fittings, their rigging went to equip small boats and those more fortunate local craft which still sailed, their deckhouses to make tool sheds and poultry sheds, their companion hatches and skylights to make seats upon the local quays.

Slowly they disintegrated, settling lower and lower in the water as their planks softened and the caulking wept from each seam. Around them in the mud there collected a host of damaged things not worth pilfering, of broken lamps and deadeyes, belaying pins, pots, pans, shattered plates and other crockery, and every kind of metal fitting. Then they ceased to float at all and were half-submerged on every tide, the salt water gushing out of them on the ebb. Their masts were taken out before they fell and heaped upon the nearby beaches and quaysides, or they were left to show, as they raked fore, aft, and athwartships, the measure of the rot within the hull. Then at last the mud entered them and, with its growing weight achieving slowly what the violence of the sea had never achieved, broke them aboard so that the deck beams ruptured and the frames split the keel length and they fell apart in their two halves fore and aft; and the stem and sternpost with hanging rudder, stood alone.

Introduction

In the quiet creeks this cycle of slow destruction was repeated many times. In Restronguet and the Ponsharden graveyard; in Pont Pill and the Padstow River: in Salcombe, the Gannell, Milford, Shannon and the southern creeks of Ireland you could find their bones lying side by side, sometimes so thick on the mud that the skeletons were piled on top of one another. Sometimes the whole hull was there. Sometimes the masts were in her. There was often nothing left except the floors of a few frames, turned iron hard, and still fastened with green bolts to the keelson. You could find wooden schooners in south Britain in every stage of disintegration. For the most part they were nameless, and often there was nobody who could tell you what they were called.

In this way half the last schooners ended. The rest were sold to Scandinavia, to trade laden with cargoes of sweet smelling Baltic soft-woods; or they were cut down to the deck level to become hulks, lying filled with other ships' cargoes, or to become barges for towing. Some were broken up, their salted timber used as fencing, or for making furniture, or for building, or burning, with yellow flames, in the cottage fires. Some were wrecked and their timbers were strewn over half the beaches of the west of England, and some of them vanished in the open sea.

A reprint from the end of The Merchant Schooners *Volume II, by permission of the author, Basil Greenhill.*

Dorset

Poole Harbour

Vessels berthed in Cobbs Quay Marina can only be satisfactorily viewed from shore, with permission from the marina office at Hamworthy. The remains of *Lady of Avenel*, *Southampton* and *Mayflower* can be visited by boat. Tidal streams are influenced by the shallows, and at springs cause a double high water. The range of tide is small, but tidal streams are strong at springs, weak at neaps. Main flood lasts about 5 hours in the harbour. There are two periods of ebb, with $7\frac{1}{2}$ hours slack water between.

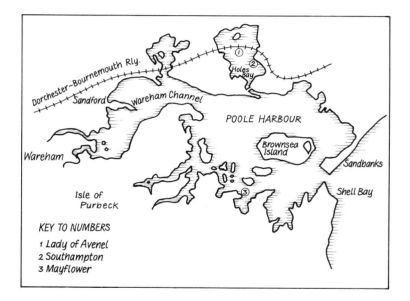

KEY TO NUMBERS

1 Lady of Avenel
2 Southampton
3 Mayflower

Brigantine *Lady of Avenel*　　　SZ 003920

The keel and ribs of this once fast and handsome vessel are only visible at low water, between the navigable channels in Holes Bay. Named after the heroine of Scott's novel *The Abbot*, she was built as a schooner at Falmouth in 1874, and three years later was sheathed for deep-sea trading. It is believed that in her early years she was engaged in the last vestiges of the then illegal slave trade. Later, she was carrying fruit from the Azores, and also ran in the Newfoundland cod trade. About 1880, when refitting in dry dock, she fell over; and while under repair was re-rigged by her owner, ED Anderton, as a brigantine. Another early mishap was the drowning of her master, knocked over-board by the main boom when altering course. Thereafter the *Lady of Avenel* was alleged to be haunted.

After the turn of the century she passed into Irish owner-ship till bought by Jenkins of Swansea in 1917. For the remainder of the Great War she was carrying Welsh coal to St Malo at £7. 10s. per ton. After hostilities, fitted with an auxiliary engine, she carried an expedition to Spitzbergen. On return, she was bought by Captain WH Dowman, who converted her to a boys' training ship, moored in Falmouth Harbour. When Captain Dowman bought the clipper *Cutty Sark*, he sold *Lady of Avenel* in 1924 to Norwegian Grettir Algarrson, who renamed her *Island* and sent her on another Arctic Expedition under Commander Frank Worsley. She was then laid up, first at Granton, then Leith, for eight years – without a caretaker, and the canvas still on her yards. During this time she was bought by Major Wright and renamed *Virgo*, but not used. In 1933 a new owner, FS Jackson, restored her original name and sailed her to Looe in Cornwall where she was converted, at considerable expense, into a yacht, without significantly altering her rig or her lines. From 1933–6 she carried her owner on cruises around the British coast, and attended the Spithead naval review in 1937. Sold to JR Hughes in 1938, she was refitted and given a new diesel engine, before taking part in the film *Sons of the Sea*, off Dartmouth. Her owner then sailed her to Poole Habour where in 1939 she was abandoned and scut-tled in Hole's Bay, after a career of 65 years. After more than 40 years of decay the wreck was blown up by the Royal Marines at the request of the Harbour Commission-ers, an operation which was largely but not wholly suc-cessful. *Lady Avenel*'s figurehead is preserved in Germany, and her binnacle in Poole Maritime Museum.

Official number : 65343. Tonnage : 214 gross, 139 net.

Mayflower — SZ 003862

Our only sighting of the *Mayflower* was from the deck of Greenslade's *Pammyann* on an Islands Cruise one August afternoon in 1986. Her timbers protruded forlornly from the water off Cleaval Point, inshore of a stake marking the navigable channel; but she dries out with the tide, when her dowelled construction can be examined. Once a sea-going schooner or ketch of about 75 tons, the *Mayflower* is thought to have come to Poole about 1919 from Plymouth. She was brought here by her owner, Tom God-den, to earn her keep as a 'teaboat'. Cruise boats running harbour trips would tie up alongside her for passengers to obtain refreshments. Tom Godden lived aboard with his wife, daughter and son for a number of years, and despite

A wreck-marker warns passing craft of Mayflower *'s last resting place, but she dries out at low water springs.* Edwina Small.

this domesticity became known to the locals as 'Robinson Crusoe'. When he gave up the teaboat service, the *Mayflower* was abandoned where she lay and has gradually disintegrated.

Ex-MFV *Vespa Star*   SZ 009898

Tidal and derelict, the grey-hulled *Vespa Star* now keeps lowly company, but it was not always thus. She can be found at the end of New Quay pier, outside some tank landing craft sunk as breakwaters, and loaded with old tyre-fenders and other junk. She is not accessible from the pier, but can be reached by boat on her port side. Built in World War II as an Admiralty Type 1001 MFV, she was afterwards sold out of the service and in the 'sixites came into the ownership of Apple, the Beatles' record-distribution company. By 1970 she was near-derelict in Poole Harbour, alongside the Power Station where she sank at her moorings. The Harbour authorities then raised her and abandoned her at New Quay pier in 1971.

Displacement: 114 tons. Length: 75·5ft × beam 19·75ft. Originally fitted with an 160hp Lister diesel. Speed: 8·5 knots.

Baltic Schooner *Stenso* (Restored and afloat)

Rigged as a tops'l schooner, the *Stenso* (Danish 'sea stone') was built in Denmark in 1901 to become one of a fleet of seven used in the trade of recovering large cubes of granite found off the Danish coast. Because of the nature of this work *Stenso* was massively built, even by Baltic trader standards. Yet her tonnage was small for a vessel of her size, because there was only one hold – a large steel tank, occupying only a small portion of the ship's capacity. The

Belying a past of murder, mystery and intrigue, Stenso *rests peacefully at Cobb's Quay.*
Edwina Small.

reason for this was the difficulty of trimming the unequal weights of the stone blocks. The ship was crewed by a master, mate and boy, and also carried two divers in forward accommodation.

Stenso was eventually sold to a British owner who laid her up in Poole. In 1974 she sank, during a gale, by Lifeboat House Steps, and the Harbour commissioners raised and moved her. She was bought by her present owner, RD Turner, in 1983. He has been thoroughly restoring her at a berth at Cobb's Quay where she can still (1987) be seen as the work nears completion. It is hoped that she will earn her keep by charter hire for sail training.

Stenso has had such a colourful career including murder, mystery and intrigue that there is a Customs File a foot thick for the Seventies alone.

Length: 60·5ft × 19·5ft. Draught 7·5ft light, 10·5ft loaded. Fitted with Burminster & Wain auxiliary engine, 115hp, in 1951.

Baltic Ketch *Katherine Jean*

A survivor of the once extensive Danish timber fleet, built in 1935. She is currently owned by Adam Ridges, who is supervising her refitting at a Cobb's Quay berth near the *Stenso*. The first break in the ship's career came when she left the timber trade to fish off Greenland. Her log books go back to the Sixties when she came into British waters and was registered at Fleetwood. In the Seventies, owned by a Mr Cato, the *Katherine Jean* once ran ashore on the Isle of Man coast and still has scars below the waterline to show for it. Adam Ridges acquired the ketch in 1983 and intends using her as a diving boat on wrecks.

Tonnage: 30 net. Length: 62·0ft × beam 18·0ft. Draught: 6·5ft

Katherine Jean *refitting as she forsakes a past of carrying timber and catching fish for a future of taking divers to wrecks.* Edwina Small.

The mystery steam tug
Southampton *abandoned since*
1955 in Poole Harbour. Edwina
Small.

Former MTB 453 as Oklahoma *on*
Green Island, nine weeks before
refloating and renaming Liberty.
Edwina Small.

Tug *Southampton* (Hulk ashore)   SZ 007915

No vessel in this survey has caused us more mystification. The wreck, a steel skeleton hull with much plating missing, lies in Hole's Bay near the new industrial road at Sterte. She does not dry out at low water. Poole Harbour Commissioners state that her name is *Southampton* and that she was abandoned in 1955. They have turned up two references in their minutes for that year.

A minute of the meeting of 24 August reads:

'Tug *Southampton*. Verbal application has been made from Mr Howard, Wicor Boatyard, Portchester, to break up the wreck of the small steel tug *Southampton* lying on the mud in Hole's Bay'.

And a minute of the meeting of 26 October reads:

'*Black Tulip* and tug *Southampton*. The owner of the hulks *Black Tulip* and *Southampton* has been advised that a guarantee will be required by the Commissioners before the above mentioned vessels are moved or broken up. To date, no reply has been received from him'.

As the wreck is still there, it must be assumed that Mr Howard never gave the guarantee and so was never given approval to remove the wreck. Records retained by the Harbour Office only date back to 1951 and they contain no other reference to the *Southampton*, but it seems probable that the vessel was brought into Hole's Bay before 1951. Enquiries through maritime publications have brought no solution as to the vessel's identity by official number. A possibility would seem to be the tug *Southampon Belle*, built at Leith in 1911 as *Muwo*, of tonnage 22 gross and 10 net. Her measurements (53·1ft × 11·5ft × 5·3ft) approximate to the apparent size of the wreck, but we can find no evidence that the *Southampton Belle* later became the *Southampton*.

MTB/Yacht *Liberty ex- Oklahoma*
(Under restoration)

When we last saw this war veteran she was hard aground on Green Island in Poole Harbour, and named *Oklahoma*. As these lines are being penned she is at Hamworthy, renamed *Liberty* and awaiting restoration. By the time this is in print, she may well be cruising through French canals.

Built by British Power Boats at Poole in 1943 as MGB 129, and converted before seeing service to MTB 453, she was then transferred, with her sisters 436 and 437, to the Royal Netherlands Navy. It is believed that she was the flotilla command ship in which Prince Bernhard of the Netherlands served. In her warship days she had 3-shaft Packard petrol engines developing 3,600bhp, and was good for 39 knots in favourable conditions. At the end of the war she was handed over to the Royal Navy and laid up in Poole Harbour.

Here she was seen by Guy and Joan Sydenham, who were seeking a floating home and purchased her. For five years they lived on her as she swung at mooring E12, and their son Russell was born on board. They then obtained a lease of Long Island and in Guy Sydenham's words: 'I put out the large bow anchor and winched the stern back on to the bank on the highest equinox tides. Here we lived happily for about 14 years. I built a small studio and finding clay in the cliff started a small salt glaze pottery'. When the family wanted to erect a wooden bungalow and move ashore, however, planning permission was refused. They were then offered a site on Green Island by its owner, and *Oklahoma* took the water again with all their possessions on board, to be towed across the harbour and run aground on Green Island's south shore. Here the bungalow was duly built and in the summer 1986 *Oklahoma* was sold to Al and Joyce Greaves, who towed her off on 2 October that year and winched her ashore at Hamworthy on a cradle they had built themselves.

Al Greaves is an enthusiast on World War II naval craft and intends to refit the vessel from stem to stern and instal new engines. She has been renamed *Liberty* and the Greaves' intention, when restoration is complete, is to take her across the Channel and cruise through the French canals to the Mediterranean. This will be resurrection indeed, for *Liberty* was last a seagoing ship in 1946, more than 40 years ago!

Tonnage: 37 displacement (as built). Length: 71·75ft × beam 20·75ft × depth 5·75ft. Original arnament: 1 2pdr, 1 twin 20mm, 2 twin .303. 2 18in torpedo tubes. Complement: 17.

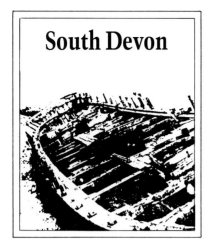

South Devon

River Exe

All the hulks in the Exe are difficult of access except the *South Coaster*, to which one can paddle – or trudge in seaboots – at low water, after crossing the railway at Cockwood. The remainder can be approached sufficiently close for photography, preferably by boat, obtainable at Exmouth.

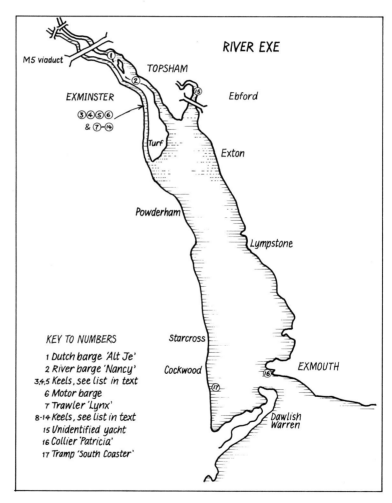

RIVER EXE

M5 viaduct

TOPSHAM

EXMINSTER

③④⑤⑥
& ⑦-⑭

Ebford

Turf

Exton

Powderham

Lympstone

KEY TO NUMBERS

1 Dutch barge 'Alt Je'
2 River barge 'Nancy'
3,4,5 Keels, see list in text
6 Motor barge
7 Trawler 'Lynx'
8-14 Keels, see list in text
15 Unidentified yacht
16 Collier 'Patricia'
17 Tramp 'South Coaster'

Starcross

Cockwood

EXMOUTH

Dawlish
Warren

Dutch barge *Alt Je* 955886

This interesting hulk is not accessible by land. A visit entails a boat expedition through an aquatic jungle of tall reeds into 'darkest Exe'. The 60 ton, ketch-rigged *Alt Je* (registered in MNL as *Altje*) was built at Nordloh, Holland, in 1905. The late WJ Newman of Topsham, who knew the ship's history, told us that she had been seized by the Navy as a suspicious vessel in 1917 and was later sold commercially. Jim Voysey recalls that she came to Topsham in the 1930s laden with cement from London, and after unloading was bought by local shipowner Dan Norton. She was then employed running from Topsham to the Isle of Wight for cement, skippered by Fred Edworthy. Later she was sold to Harry Wannell of Topsham who installed a 4-cylinder Kelvin engine and ran her from Dartmouth to Exeter with gravel. Her skipper was then Richard Jewell, known locally as 'Dick the Greek'. Worn out at last, the *Alte Je* was abandoned in this reedy leat at the end of the sewerage works peninsula, and became tidal. Towering reeds now hide her from public review as, filled with mud, she rots peacefully away and reverts to nature.

Official number: 139069. Tonnage: 59 gross, 33 net. Length: 70·2ft × beam 18·0ft × 6·6ft. Engine: 28ihp.

River Exe (West Bank)

Barge *Nancy* SY 960882

Just outside the disused Topsham Lock on the Exeter Ship Canal is the fairly complete hulk of the wooden barge *Nancy*. She is wall-sided, double-ended and has tiller steering. Her working life was spent locally, and her owners were Exeter City Council.

Barge Nancy *at Topsham Lock.*

Trawler *Lynx* SY 964877

The hulk of the trawler *Lynx* lies amid the rushes on the marshy bank between the Exeter Ship Canal and the River Exe, opposite Topsham. Most of her after-frames have collapsed around the keelson, but enough remains of the forepart of the ship, and her sternpost, to proclaim her Brixham trawler pedigree instantly to the visitor.

The *Lynx*, sloop-class and ketch-rigged, was built in 1903 by JW & A Upham, under foreman Crouch for the fleet of usually seven or eight trawlers which the ship builders operated themselves. She had a square stern, a keel length of 66ft, and cost £560. Carrying the portmark BM 217, she was one of the largest sailing trawlers working out of Brixham.

Lynx was a strong contender annually in the Regatta, and on one occasion was involved in an incident which was a point of dispute among fishermen for long after. She came into collision with the famous *Erycina* of Plymouth, which, skippered by Johnny Taylor, had overtaken her and was crossing her bows. The Plymouth boat lodged a strong protest, but the *Lynx*'s handling was not faulted by the arbitrators. Upham's sold her in the 1920s to owner/skipper John Tidmarsh and she continued trawling from Brixham until 1931. She then changed hands again, going

The bows of the trawler Lynx *against the backdrop of Topsham waterfront.* Edwina Small.

to Cornish owners at Mousehole. This last phase of her working life barely lasted a year, and her registry entry was cancelled 15 October 1932 when it was reported that she was sold for breaking.

How she came to rest her bones on the Exe is not clear. In the years between the Wars, the trawlers of fishermen bankrupted by loss of gear on sunken wrecks were sometimes bought by Topsham men, who cut big hatches and used them for coasting. The *Lynx* may have been reprieved from the breakers with this intention, but it is reasonably certain that after arrival in the Exe she did not put to sea again.

To reach the *Lynx* from Exminster, leave the A379 to cross the railway at the site of the former Exminster station. Continue to the right-hand turn where the footpath to canal and ferry is visible, in a field. Park on the verge of the lane, and take the footpath. The approach along the river/canal bank is rough going. From Topsham, park by the quay and take the ferry.

Official number: 114248. Tonnage: 53·28 gross, 46·67 net. Length: 70·2ft × beam 18·1ft × moulded depth 9·1ft.

A Row of Keels and Wreckage   SY 964877

From a distance only the *Lynx* and a steel barge can be seen. In fact however there are keels and other remains of 12 vessels on this bank but separate identification is now scarcely possible. Two local ex-mariners who now, sadly, have passed on, but whom we consulted some years ago, agreed on the following names; and that the following order, from north to south, is probably correct:

Topsham ex-*Oliver* Trow. ON 63087 1871 63 tons reg.
Mistletoe Sail trawler. ON 93983 1890 46 tons reg.
Leader Barquentine. ON 60660 1869 185 tons reg.
Un-named steel motor barge. No details known.
Lynx Sail trawler (qv).
Commander Sail trawler. ON 110808 1899 47 tons reg.
Harewood Ketch. No details known.
Belle Smack. ON 5706 1855 35 tons reg.
Lynher Smack. No details known. Not to be confused with Tamar barge.
Friendship Sail trawler. ON 117462 1903 49 tons net.
Smilin' Morn Sail trawler. ON 93855 1886 43 tons net.
Tentative Ketch. No details known.

There are said to be three more hulks on the opposite east bank, all now buried under the concrete of Trite's boatyard.

Emerald Smack. ON 5701 1835 38 tons reg.
Rescue Sail trawler. ON 90961 1886 45 tons reg.
and a coastal collier, details not known.

Gaunt remains of the South Coaster *in Starcross Bight.* Edwina Small.

Steam tramp *South Coaster*   SY 980804

The conspicuous hulk off Cockwood in the Exe estuary is the steam tramp *South Coaster*, which invariably interests passengers on mainline trains running through Starcross. She was a Cardiff collier which met her end during World War II; not however, as a victim of enemy attack, but, ironically, as a result of attempts to avoid such a fate. In 1943 she was bound from Marsden, near South Shields , for Exeter, with a cargo of 'Yorkshire hards', and was hugging the unlighted coast to avoid a U-boat encounter. On December 13 she ran aground on the eastern extremity of Pole Sands off Exmouth – so near and yet so far. A steam tug and a landing craft were hurried to the scene by the Navy, but the collier was 'hard and fast' and resisted all attempts to move her.

The crew of the Exmouth lifeboat stood by on shore while the Navy kept up the efforts to tow the *South Coaster* off the bank, and for eight days following a watchful eye was kept on the weather. On December 21 a sou'-sou' westerly gale sprang up and the Navy summoned the lifeboat. The RNLI *Catherine Harriet Eaton* launched into heavy seas, and with some difficulty got alongside the wreck and took off the ship's company of 13. The *South Coaster* now took a hammering from the weather, and it became clear that her days as a seagoing ship were numbered.

With the return of less boisterous weather, the Navy resumed salvage attempts, and after off-loading some cargo, they succeeded in getting the collier afloat again. However, she was making water badly and was clearly damaged beyond economical repair. She was therefore towed, with pumps working furiously, into the River Exe, and allowed to settle on the mud clear of the fairway. There she lies today, less than 100 yards from the railway embankment at Starcross, an object of unfailing interest to train passengers for over 40 years. In this position she was unloaded, and all fittings of value salvaged. Since then she has been cut down by scrap merchants, and her engines dismantled.

Today she is a sorry sight, only her mainmast, bridge and forepeak showing above water at most stages of the tide. At low water springs only her bow is immersed, and it is possible to walk out over the sand and board her. Her starb'd side has largely given way, and no. 2 bulkhead has collapsed. Her stern plating is missing, but the rusting propellor shaft (minus screw) is still in place.

Some years ago railway passengers and passers-by ashore were astonished to see a briefly-clad female form clinging to the mast. Assistance for the presumed stranded yachtswoman was not slow in forthcoming, but the would-be rescuers found only a milliners' dummy, and the wag who perpetrated the joke has never been discovered!

The collier's hull is now silted up with mud and sand and heavily encrusted with mussels. Her plates are mysteriously holed in several places: it seems most probably that this was done to expedite draining at low water during the salvage operations.

Official number: 162122. Built: 1916. Tonnage: 513 gross. Length: 159·4ft × beam 25·7ft × depth 11·9ft.

River Exe (East Bank)

Unknown Yacht   SY 976877

Between Topsham and Exton the east bank of the Exe is interrupted by the tributary River Clyst, which is spanned by the Exeter-Exmouth railway. On the Clyst's east bank, above the railway viaduct, lies the hulk of a yacht, under overhanging trees. Much of the decking and hull planking has been removed. All our enquiries to establish her identity have failed.

Stern and displaced rudder of the Patricia *under Exmouth Dock Jetty.* Les Hill.

Collier *Patricia*   SY 994806

The remains of this vessel are easier to locate than they are to see, since they are mostly submerged except at low water.

The *Patricia* was an iron-hulled sailing collier, a class of vessel of which no example has been preserved. She plied in the English and Bristol channels, and was owned by the late Commander Adams of Exmouth, who married the Lady Waldron.

Retired from service after the Great War and hulked, the *Patricia* was acquired about 1920 by the Exmouth Dock Company for a breakwater and jetty at the western side of the dock entrance. She was manoeuvred into position on a falling tide, grounded at low water, holed, and bolted to upright piles. Since then, the tide scouring has caused the seaward end of the hulk to be depressed: so the vessel's remains, once on an even keel, now lie at an angle, and even at low water only the stern at the shoreward end is usually visible. Retired Exmouth pilot Harold (Dido) Bradford remembers the hulk being positioned. Some years ago the jetty over the wreck was rebuilt and shortened, and it may be that some of the seaward end of the hulk was then cut away.

Official number: 132894. Built: 1913. Tonnage: 781 gross. Length: 122·7ft × beam 30·6ft × depth: 12·5ft.

Donnatoo *ex*-Brighter Hope – *the unwelcome yet hapless guest at Dawlish Warren.* Edwina Small.

Fishing lugger *Donnatoo* SY 993802

Hard ashore at the north-eastern extremity of Dawlish Warren lies the wooden auxiliary fishing lugger *Donnatoo*, portmark E 290. Although the local authority have demanded her removal, and despite a notice on her bulwark proclaiming that she is under repair, it appears unlikely that she will put to sea again, and is now tidal. Norwegian built, at Flekkefjord in 1943, she was previously named *Brighter Hope*, and fished from Lerwick in Scotland, with the portmark LK 241. In the Sixties, it is believed, she came south to Padstow, re-registered as PW 119. She was then purchased by the late Tom Litton of Lympstone, but continued to fish the Cornish coast from Exmouth, where she was re-registered as E 290 on September 4, 1984. The story persists that she is the fishing vessel which early in 1985 was in the national news after having her nets entangled by a surfacing submarine, and losing her gear; but we have not been able to substantiate this. On the lower half of a tide one can walk round the derelict after a short boat trip from Exmouth beach or a half-hour stroll along the Warren sand dunes.

Tonnage: 21·8 gross and net. Length: 49·9ft (OA), 47·5ft (BP) × beam 17·0ft × depth 6·0ft.

Girl Kate

The older generation may wonder what became of the Exe's best-remembered hulk, the *Girl Kate*. This former schooner converted to houseboat was for long a conspicuous landmark on Dawlish Warren. The vessel lay between the golf courses and the sand dunes at the eastern end, and there was much speculation as to how she got there. The *Girl Kate* was said to have been a salvaged vessel bought by George Abell of Exmouth and towed by cargo boat to a former inlet of the Warren known as 'the creek', about 1919; and then hauled across the sand by a team of horses. Latterly she was occupied by an Exmouth antiques dealer named Steer, who had come here to be near the golf course. In the late Thirties a two-day gale coinciding with spring tides swept away much of the east Warren and imperilled the *Girl Kate*. During World War II troops used the unoccupied hulk for target practice. The end came in December 1946 when a combination of heavy rain, spring tides and a strong sou'easterly gale assailed the Warren. The railway line at Cockwood was undermined, Warren bungalows were demolished and the remains of *Girl Kate* were swept away. No trace can be seen today.

A girl named Monica holds the foreground but behind her in 1930 rests the now-vanished Girl Kate. Obelisk Publications.

Lowly vessel with majestic pedigree: Bertha *the Brunel-designed dredger at Exeter.* Exeter Maritime Museum.

Dredger *Bertha* (Afloat and restored)
Exeter Maritime Museum

The name *Bertha* appears defiantly above these notes, because although this humble yet remarkable craft has never officially been dignified by a name, nor carried one on her hull, *Bertha* is the name by which she has long been affectionately known. *Bertha* is a harbour dredger, and has the distinction of being the oldest operating steam craft in Britain – and possibly in the world. She is believed to have been designed by Isambard K Brunel, and the year that she was built, 1844, was the year in which his revolutionary steamship *Great Britain* was commissioned.

Bertha was built by Lunel's of Bristol, a firm that went out of business two years later. She was assembled in Bridgwater, Somerset, where the whole of her working life was to be spent, keeping the docks free of mud and silt. Her system of dredging appears primitive but was apparently effective. A square-sectioned vertical rod over the vessel's stern controls a broad metal blade under the water. The blade was lowered into the mud and the dredger then hauled itself along by a drag-chain. As it did so, the blade dragged the mud with it, eventually dragging it into the stream of the River Parrett, where the current dispersed it and completed the task. The steam engine which hauled on the drag-chain is single-cylinder and double-acting, and works at a pressure of 40 psi.

The Museum accepted *Bertha* as a gift from British Rail, and the Transport Trust met the cost of her transportation by road from Bridgwater Docks to Exeter.

Gross tonnage: 63·4. Length: 50·0ft × beam 14·0ft × depth 4·0ft.

Pilot Cutter *Cariad*
(Afloat and restored) Exeter Maritime Museum

Cariad was the last of the sailing pilot cutters to work in the difficult waters of the Bristol Channel. She was built, of pitch-pine on oak, at Pill near Bristol in 1904; but registered and based at Cardiff, where she worked for 14 years carrying pilots to ships making for the ports in the Bristol Channel. This was a testing environment, and the competition on the pilotage business was very keen: if the pilots knew of a particular vessel bound for a Bristol Channel port they would often sail round Land's End into the English Channel to intercept her. The cutters therefore had to be well-found sea-keeping craft, able to sail well to windward, and yet be handled by a minimum crew of two men. *Cariad* fulfilled all these requirements. The seas of the Bristol Channel can be short and steep, and the prevailing wind is sou'westerly, so the best-found boats secured the 'plum' jobs.

In 1918 *Cariad* was transferred to Bristol, where for four years she was the last pilot cutter in full-time service under sail. In 1922 she was replaced by a motor cutter, withdrawn from pilot service, and sold for conversion to a yacht. For 31 years, from 1926 to 1957, she was owned by Frank Carr, who was director of the National Maritime Museum from 1947–66 and was the moving spirit behind the restoration of the clipper *Cutty Sark*. He sold *Cariad* in 1957 but in 1971 negotiated the purchase of the boat on behalf of Exeter Maritime Museum, and personally sailed her from Gravesend to Exeter.

Here she was craned out of the water and volunteers at the Museum erected a weather canopy over her and began restoration work. This was inhibited by lack of funds and in 1984 she was transported by road to Torpoint ballast pond in the Port of Plymouth, where she was craned into the hold of an ex-Admiralty ammunition lighter. A roof was built over the hold and restoration work began again, under the supervision of Phil Risby, head of Plymouth Community Boatyard Project. Twenty-five part-time workers were employed and the work was funded by the Manpower Services Commission.

The restoration has involved the replacement of some frames and about half the floors; considerable repair to the yellow-pine deck, and the fitting of a new rudder. A 1½-ton spruce trunk from Denmark was obtained for

As she was and as she will be: Cariad *the pilot cutter.* Model Ship Dockyard.

fashioning into a new 65ft mast, and a new suit of four white cotton sails has been provided. Eight sleeping berths are being installed in the former pilots' cabin, as the *Cariad* is to begin a new life taking young people adventure sailing.

Gross tonnage: 18·09. Length: 42·5ft × beam 12·5ft × depth 7·4ft.

Steam tug *St Canute*
(Afloat and restored) Exeter Maritime Museum

The *St Canute*, Danish-built in 1931, has not the thrustful, no-nonsense symmetry of the typical British tug; she is, somehow, more flamboyant. Nor does she possess the trim lines of *Portwey*, the first steam tug to be preserved in Devon,* because aesthetically she is over-funnelled. Nevertheless, *St Canute* is a fine example of multi-purpose ship design, being equipped for fire-fighting and ice-breaking as well as towage: and certainly she is a prime attraction to visitors at the Exeter Maritime Museum. She was built at Frederikshavns, Denmark, and spent the greater part – 29 years – of her working life at Odense,

A prime attraction of Exeter's Maritime Museum – St Canute *the Danish-built steam tug.* Edwina Small.

where she was known as *St Knud*, and fulfilled all three purposes for which she was designed.

She was sold in 1960 to the Fowey Harbour Commissioners, and was employed as reserve tug for berthing freighters coming to load china clay. The work at Fowey was insufficient to keep her continually in steam and the constant heating and cooling process of raising steam and drawing fires was detrimental to her boiler and making her uneconomic. The Commissioners therefore advertised her for sale, and with steam tugs everywhere being displaced by diesel, it seemed that she was destined for the breakers.

She was saved from this fate by Mr Armstrong Evans of Trebullet, Cornwall, who with two partners purchased *St Canute* at a favourable price from the Harbour Commissioners, who were sympathetic to the preservation project. Her new owners arranged to lend her to the Exeter Maritime Museum, but considerable care was needed to bring her to the basin, for at the lower gates of Double Locks on the Exeter Ship Canal she had less than an inch to spare on either side, while her 10ft 6in draught was the maximum permitted in the canal.

St Canute is periodically steamed each summer, and is maintained in full working order. The officers' saloon and cabins, crew's quarters, galley and wheelhouse are all open to the public. Her main engine is triple-expansion reciprocating, of 500ihp and her Scotch wet-back return-tube boiler is coal fired in twin furnaces. She is equipped with a powerful pump for fire-fighting and her reinforced bows are designed to ride up over ice and crush it.

Tonnage: 92·83 gross. Length: (BP) 86·1ft × beam 25·1ft × depth 11·7ft.

*Now at St Katharine's Dock, London.

Former Teignmouth lifeboat Henry Finlay, *returning from a service under tow.* Author's collection.

Passenger Launch *Henrietta*
(Afloat and in service)

This former RNLI lifeboat is maintained by her owner Peter Hockings in first-class condition, and is a rewarding sight for shiplovers' eyes. Built in 1911 by the Thames Iron Works, Blackwall, at a cost of £930, she was originally named *Henry Finlay*, after the London mechant from whose bequest to the RNLI she had been provided. She was a standard 35-foot self-righting type pulling and sailing lifeboat, and served 'till 1930 at Macrihanish, Argyllshire, when the station was closed.

The *Henry Finlay* came south in 1930 to replace the *Alfred Staniforth* as the lifeboat for Teignmouth, where she served 'till 1940. On 16 August 1931 she went to the gale-lashed schooner *Myonie R. Kirby* of London and landed an injured crewman. On 17 March 1937 she was launched to assist a small boat, *Betsy* of Teignmouth, which was sinking, and saved the owner's life.

Teignmouth lifeboat station was closed in World War II and the *Henry Finlay* was purchased by a local boatowner and renamed *Teignmouth Belle*, being used for summer 'trips in the bay' and winter fishing, with an engine installed. Years later she was sold to D Rackley of Dawlish for similar work and renamed *Victoria*.

Peter Hockings bought her in 1984, renamed her *Henrietta* after his mother, and repainted her in lifeboat colouring. He runs summer excursions from Exmouth Beach which have proved immensely popular with children on holiday. In April 1986 *Henrietta* took part in an RNLI Medical Exercise off the mouth of the Exe, and Peter Hockings was congratulated by the SW lifeboats inspector on his boat's magnificent condition.

Tonnage: 3·5 gross. Length: 35·0ft × beam 9·6ft × depth 3·0ft. Length overall: *c* 38ft. Fitted with 75hp Ford D engine.

River Teign

The Teign has a very strong ebb and is not a place for the novice. However, a boat is really of no advantage in visiting either hulk, as the *Two Brothers* lies only yards from the B 3195 and can be reached, wearing seaboots, at low water: while the *Karrie* can be approached in the same way, though with more difficulty, from Passage House Inn, Kingsteignton.

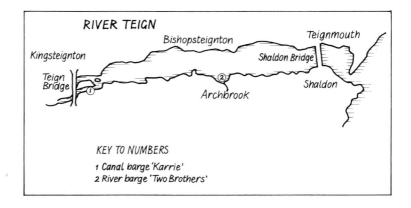

The Karrie *rotting quietly away amid the grassy mudflats of the Teign.* Edwina Small.

Karrie   SX 880723

Since the opening of the eleven-span Teign Bridge carrying the Kingsteignton and Newton Abbot bypass, the gaunt timbers of the *Karrie* have been a familiar sight to motorists on the A 380. She lies in the marshes at the head of the Teign navigation. filled and emptied by every tide.

Karrie was a Stover Canal barge and one of the last craft to carry the ancient Norse rig of a single square sail on a mast stepped well for'ard. Built at Gerry's onetime boatyard on the canal, at a date no longer recorded, the *Karrie* was originally one of Watts, Black & Bearns fleet of barges, which were distinguished by white-painted bulwarks, and is said to have been named after the daughter of one of the directors. The *Karrie* ferried ball clay to Teignmouth harbour for shipment until about 1935 when she was sold, with two other barges, to Mr F Hoyse of Kingsteignton who used them for river-sand transport. By boat, the now-disintegrated remains of the *Karrie* can only be approached near to high tide, when she is largely under water. To examine her construction it is necessary to wade in high boots from the bank at Passage House Inn.

Karrie's two sister barges still exist – out of sight! One was sunk beside the NE bank of the Whitelake Channel, Newton Abbot, to create a 'narrows' and discourage silting. Her remains have sunk into the mud, position SX 865718. The other was lying derelict in a gut on the south side of Stover Canal at Jetty Marsh. This gut was filled in years ago by tipping, and the barge, which was capable of restoration, buried at the same time, position SX 863720.

No specific details of the *Karrie* are available, but the average dimensions of the Stover barges were 56ft × 13ft 6in with a load capacity of 30 tons of ball clay on a draught of 3ft for'ard and 3ft 9in aft.

Seen through the hedge at Combe-in-Teignhead road, the Two Brothers *at Archbrook.* Martin Langley.

Two Brothers   SX 908723

The motorised sand barge *Two Brothers* led a humble and in the main uneventful life on the waters of the Teign: but she has a pedigree, for she was built by Upham's of Brixham, in August 1924; and her present resting-place at Archbrook is a quiet and beautiful spot, lending dignity to her retirement. Here the B 3195 Shaldon to Combe-in-Teignhead road crosses a brook at its meeting with the river, and the motorist can draw up on the sandy shore.

For most of her working life the *Two Brothers* was owned by Noyse Bros of Newton Abbot, and was named after the partners Frank and Fred. She plied with sand between Jetty Marsh on the Stover Canal and Teignmouth harbour quays. She was always well maintained, getting a thorough annual overhaul on an improvised slip at

Two Brothers, a recent picture showing further disintegration due to vandalism. Edwina Small.

The Golden Hind *at Brixham in 1978. In November 1987, whilst on passage to Dartmouth for a refit, a leak developed due to shrunk planking and she sank off Stoke Fleming. Salvaged, her owner proposes to restore her at a cost of £100,000 and return her to Brixham.*

Hackney Marsh. Here she was fitted with a powerful 14hp Kelvin engine. Later the *Two Brothers* and the river-sand business was taken over by Foster's, a local concern: then resold after a few years to the Devon Concrete Company of Barnstaple. Her working days eventually over, this company removed her engine and propeller and beached her in Archbrook creek. Here she was visited in the seventies by the late Commander McKie who took off her lines in scale drawings for posterity.

Length: 41·3ft × beam 13·5ft × depth 4·5ft. Built of oak on an elm bottom.

Brixham Harbour

Replica *Golden Hind* ex-*Centurion*
(Afloat and operational)   926563

This approximate replica of the ship in which Drake circumnavigated the world is berthed at the Fish Quay in Brixham, and is open to the public throughout the summer months.

(The original *Golden Hind* was built, probably at Deptford, in the first half of the 16th century, and called *Pelican* until renamed by Drake during the homeward run of his epic voyage. She was a ship of about 110 (contemporary tons), with approximate measurements of 90ft length, 17ft beam, and 9ft depth in hold. Designed for merchant service and not as a warship, she had no gun deck as such, but carried 18 cannon on her world voyage. By order of Queen Elizabeth the *Golden Hind* was afterwards laid up in dry dock at Deptford 'as a monument for all posterity' and for years was one of the sights of London. Little was done however to preserve her from the depredetions of time, weather and souvenir hunters, and sadly this national treasure was eventually broken up in the 17th century).

The replica in Brixham Harbour began life in 1940 as a 70ft (OA) Admiralty MFV with a diesel engine, and after service in World War II was abandoned on the mud at Rosyth. But a new lease of life awaited her.

In 1950 she was acquired by the SPG* missionary society for a special project to mark their 250th anniversary the next year. Mr JD Dixon of the Society sailed her from Rosyth to Brightlingsea. There she was converted to a replica of the 17th/18th century warship HMS *Centurion*, in which the first missionary sent out by SPG on behalf of the Church of England sailed in 1701 to America. The conversion was carried out by Messrs James & Co, and involved the adding of an outer hull. With the services of an experienced naval architect and invaluable help from the National Maritime Museum, the ship became a half-scale replica (scale in terms of overall length) of the original *Centurion*. From June 1951 to October 1952 she visited English seaports and the Channel Islands as a floating mission centre and exhibition.

In 1961 Transcontinental Films bought the ship for use in a TV series on Sir Francis Drake, and she was converted to a replica of *Golden Hind* at Flushing, Falmouth – although her MFV engine was retained. The filming over, the ship was abandoned on the banks of the Thames.

In 1964 a private company took her over, restored her, improved her authenticity as a replica, and removed her engine. She was then sailed in Torbay for an American film, in May 1965. Later that year she was sold to John Lee, her present owner, under whose care her interior was made as authentic as knowledge of the original permits. The ship was then berthed in Brixham on public display. At the end of the summer season 1977 a fire broke out on board which severely damaged the after-end of the interior. Repairs cost £50,000 but in 1978 the ship was hired by the BBC for the making of a two-hour film on the Pilgrim Fathers, starring Edward Fox. For this purpose she was temporarily altered to resemble the *Mayflower*, and scenes of the colonisation of America were recreated in the abandoned quarry below Berry Head.

Although not a perfect replica, the *Golden Hind* at Brixham used to be well worth a visit. Unfortunately she sunk on tow in 1987 and a question mark hangs over her future.

Official number: 184512. Port of Registry, London.

In the guise of HMS Centurion *the former MFV, later to become the replica* Golden Hind, *at York in 1953.*

*Society for the Propagation of the Gospel.

River Dart

Separate instructions are given for reaching the various hulks and ship-remains, which are widely dispersed all over the estuary.

Small boats (motor or oar) may be hired at Dartmouth Quay and Greenway Quay, in the summer; while a number of the derelicts can be seen and photographed from the river excursion boats operating from Dartmouth Quay. If hiring a boat, you would be wise not to enter the creeks on a falling tide.

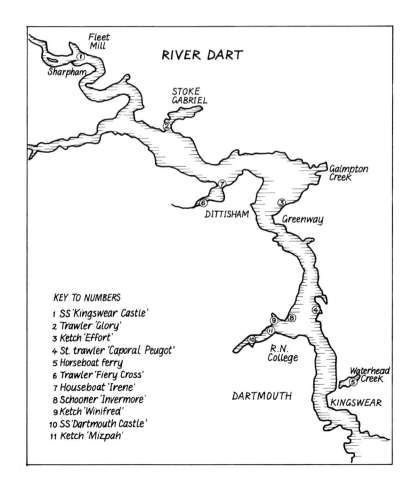

RIVER DART

Fleet Mill

Sharpham

STOKE GABRIEL

Galmpton Creek

DITTISHAM

Greenway

R.N. College

Waterhead Creek

DARTMOUTH

KINGSWEAR

KEY TO NUMBERS
1 SS 'Kingswear Castle'
2 Trawler 'Glory'
3 Ketch 'Effort'
4 St. trawler 'Caporal Peugot'
5 Horseboat ferry
6 Trawler 'Fiery Cross'
7 Houseboat 'Irene'
8 Schooner 'Invermore'
9 Ketch 'Winifred'
10 SS 'Dartmouth Castle'
11 Ketch 'Mizpah'

River Dart (East Bank)

SS *Kingswear Castle*   SX 828583

A rusting paddle-steamer hull on the mud at Fleet Mill Creek, *Kingswear Castle* (1) was built of steel by Cox & Company of Falmouth in 1904. She was the fourth purpose-built excursion steamer acquired by the River Dart Steamboat Company. For 10 years, until the coming of the *Compton Castle* in 1914, she was the largest on the river and pride of the fleet. Those were the balmy years when passenger traffic justified the building of new vessels. *Kingswear Castle* and her consorts were on the river only half as long as the succeeding four steamers which all ran for 40 or more years and saw the decline of the Company. Her career lasted until 1924, when she was hulked to become a fever-ship for a few years, after removal of her engines. These were installed in the ship of the same name which replaced her. (*Kingswear Castle* (2) was withdrawn in 1965 but was acquired by the Paddle Steamer Preservation Society and has been fully restored. She now operates on the Thames and Medway, still using these now 83-year-old engines!) *Kingswear Castle* (1) was finally put ashore here at Fleet Mill.

Since then, thousands of passengers on Dart excursion boats have had her pointed out to them by the commentator; but invariably she is mistakenly described as *Dartmouth Castle*, while in ECB Thornton's *South Coast Pleasure Steamers* she is given as *Berry Castle*. In 1974 she was daubed conspicuously with the name *Anton Bres*, a disfigurement which the harbour authority plans to remove. This was the result of youthful adventure one night when the young engineer from a Bres Line coaster bringing timber to Totnes decided to 'leave his mark'.

To reach this hulk by land, turn from the Stoke Gabriel – Aish – Longcombe Road near Parliament Cottage and take the lane to Fleet Mill Farm. Here one must seek permission to cross farm land to the river bank. To reach the *Kingswear Castle* by water, use a small-draught motor-boat, and time arrival for just before high water. Steer straight for the conduit and when opposite the wreck's stern go 90° to port and make fast to the starboard bow.

Tonnage: 85 gross, 47 net. Length: 107·6ft × beam 15·1ft × moulded depth 5·0ft. Engines: 2-cyl compound. Speed about 8 knots.

Trawler *Glory*   SX 847567

The remains of the sailing trawler *Glory* lie on the foreshore of Stoke Gabriel creek. This is a much-visited beauty

Once she fished the English Channel: now a playground for children. Glory *at Stoke Gabriel.* Martin Langley.

Familiar but anonymous to many Dartmouth holidaymakers, the hulk at Greenway. Is this the Effort*?* Edwina Small.

spot, and *Glory*'s gaunt timbers must be well known – albeit anonymously – to many holidaymakers, who enjoy the pebbly walk under the trees to the mouth of the creek. A few pause to consider what kind of vessel this may once have been been, invariably deciding 'just a barge', while their children jump into the pebble-filled bilge and pretend they are afloat.

The *Glory* was an intermediate Brixham trawler of the 'mule' class, built in 1906 by Sanders and Galmpton for an owner-skipper named Ellis. Her Brixham fishing post-mark was BM 16. Ellis was a very devout man, and·it is said that he originally named his new trawler *Glory for me*. There were many devout Christian trawlermen in those times, whose forebears had been influenced by the preaching of John Wesley and it was invariable for Brixham smacks to return to harbour on Saturday evening and not sail until Monday morning – a respect for the Lord's Day which was to last throughout the days of the sail fleet. *Glory* proved herself a fast vessel and several times won the King George V Cup at the annual Brixham regatta. She was certainly still trawling in the twenties.

In 1929 she was auctioned at Brixham quay – without her spars – to Lieut Commander Bewley RNR and converted to a houseboat. On the eve of August Bank Holiday, 1932, she parted a shackle of cable in an easterly gale and grounded in Paignton at the top of the springs. She was refloated, little damaged, six weeks later. Within a year of this mishap *Glory* was towed to the River Dart and sold to a former owner of Pontin's camps as a floating adjunct to a holiday camp. Insecurely moored, she went adrift in 1938 and sustained hull damage which made repair uneconomic. She was salvaged by local rivermen, and propped up at Stoke Gabriel in her present position, and has since gradually decayed.

Official number: 122881. Tonnage: 34·14 gross, 25·55 net. Ketch rig, square stern. Length: 62·5ft × beam 15·5ft moulded depth 7·6ft.

Is this the *Effort*? SX 871550

This hulk, which I believe to be the ketch *Effort*, is easy of access, for she lies under the trees about 200 yards above the Greenway Ferry quay. You can park your car on the quay and provided it is not high water, you can walk along the foreshore.

For years this hulk's identity has been a mystery to visitors and longshoremen alike. On the Dart pleasure-craft she has often been confidently pointed out to passengers as 'an old Brixham trawler'. But a Brixham trawler she most certainly is not. She is a little too long for the largest 'sloop' class; the timber strakes of her hull are too narrow; she has a different hull form below the waterline; there is no port cut in the bows for the bowsprit: and the design of her stern is untypical of Brixham trawlers. We have measured the hulk and her length × beam × depth figures approximate quite closely to those of the ketch *Effort*, which is known to have been abandoned in the Dart. Precise comparison is not possible as the hulk has opened out in the beam and flattened in the bilges after years of dereliction. However, after research and enquiries over two years, we feel reasonably sure that this hulk is the remains of the ketch *Effort*, built by William Date of Kingsbridge as long ago as 1880.

Lloyd's Register for 1912–13 records her owners as H Grant & Co and her port of registry as Salcombe. Nothing can be traced of her early history, but almost certainly she was engaged in general coastwise trading and at the low rates then paid for such cargoes, affording her crew a somewhat meagre living and hard life. Ultimately she was acquired by the Langmeads of Galmpton and together with the *Mizpah* (qv) – which now lies two miles away on the other side of the river – was employed carrying sand and gravel from the Dart to Torbay, during the

Happier days. Langmead's ketches Mizpah *and* Effort *in Torquay harbour, date unknown.* Automatic Printing Company.

enlargement of Torquay harbour. For this work she was fitted with an engine, and the outer end of the shaft piping is still visible. It is not known whether the *Effort* was sold or laid up when Langmeads replaced her and the *Mizpah* by a steam barge which had the latest dredging equipment.

In World War II she was moored in the Dart as a balloon/barrage vessel, and the modification to her bows for this purpose can still be seen. Whilst performing this humble duty, she was the victim of a near-miss by a German aircraft which 'started' her planking. Repair was considered uneconomic and she was run ashore in her present position, where beachcombers have vandalised her hull to obtain timber.

Official number: 81757. Tonnage: 65 gross and net. Length: 67·7ft × beam 18·6ft × depth 8·2ft.

Trawler *Caporal Peugot*   SX 879529

Although I have boldly headed this paragraph *Caporal Peugot*, the identity of the hulk concerned is not completely proven, despite extensive researches. She lies on Noss Beach, part of Philip & Son's shipyard property. The harbour authority has no record of the ship's identity, nor of the date when she entered harbour.

She is a French wooden steam trawler, with all superstructure and most fittings removed from her main deck and her engine space open to the sky. Despite her French ownership when she came to the Dart, the National Maritime Museum believe she may have been built at Lowestoft or in Scotland. She probably came into the river in 1940, but has lain on this beach since 1945; and some years ago she appeared for a short while in a TV commercial. Some repair work was done on her in 1945 under

The mystery Frenchman at Lower Noss beach. Almost certainly this is the Dunkirk veteran Caporal Peugot. *Edwina Small.*

an Admiralty Order, but it was evidently abandoned, perhaps due to a mishap, as the interior of the hull shows there has been a fire. When the vessel was deemed a 'total constructive loss' Philip's were asked if she could be abandoned on their land as she lay. Permission was given because the hulk helped retain the mud and prevent further erosion. The vessel's main beam is missing so her identity cannot be ascertained from her official number.

The Musee de la Marine, Paris, however, consider that the available evidence points to her being the *Caporal Peugot*, which is known to have been at Noss in the 1940s when her 2-cylinder compound engines were partly dismantled for overhaul. She is shown in Lenton and Colledge's *Warships of World War II* (Ian Allan 1964) as returned to owners, but this is incorrect. *Caporal Peugot* had been requisitioned by the French Government as auxiliary minesweeper AD 9 under the command of Bos'n Josselin, in 1939. She was working from Dunkirk at the time of the German offensive in May, 1940. The following month she was at Cherbourg, assisting to evacuate French and British troops encircled by Rommel's panzers. On June 17, as a result of engine damage, she was in tow of the *L'Andre Louis*, heading for Aberwrac'h, but with the fall of Brest imminent, the corvette group with which she was in company made for Plymouth, where it is believed she was taken over by the Royal Navy.

She is deteriorating rapidly, but has the pleasing lines of every thoroughbred trawler and this corner of the Dart will be the poorer when she disintegrates. With telescopic lens she can be photographed from the road above, or from the passing Dart excursion boats; but she is on private land and permission to board her would not be granted in view of her condition.

Horseboat SX 887514

In Waterhead Creek is a survivor of the horseboats used on the Lower Ferry in the days of Casey & Heal ownership. It is hidden by trees from the road and you must walk the south foreshore to find it. This float, originally propelled by sweeps, was later towed by the steam pinnace *Forester*. It could transport two carts and horses.

River Dart (West Bank)

Two Nameless Belgians SX 834565

In Bow Creek, near the bottom of the footpath from Cornworthy, lie the wooden hulls of two unidentified Belgian trawlers. These are two of eight Belgian boats which were

The hulks of two unknown Belgian trawlers at Bow Creek in Spring 1980.

fishing from Brixham at the outbreak of World War II and were interned as a security measure. A Belgian caretaker visited the vessels daily via the Duncannon Ferry to carry out routine maintenance. Eventually six of the boats were handed back to the Belgians but these two which were in poor condition – one of them holed – have lain here ever since.

Trawler *Fiery Cross*   SX 854552

At the head of Dittisham Greek, where the lane from Cornworthy runs briefly beside the water before climbing to Dittisham village, the remains of the trawler *Fiery Cross* lie in disarray upon a mudbank. The sternpost still rises from her keel, but the rudder, with a pintle broken, hangs askew. Slowly disintegrating, the *Fiery Cross* has lain here since 1937.

She was built by J Bowden at Porthleven in 1905 for the Ramsgate trawl fleet of Mr Paynter who owned several boats similarly named, including *Rosy Cross* and *Crimson Cross*. With the portmark R 291 she fished from Ramsgate until U-boat activity in the Great War on the east coast caused her, with other Ramsgate boats, to transfer to Brixham. She never returned to the east coast and in 1923 was advertised for sale by shipbroker Barney Easton of Swansea, and bought by skipper Harry Davie of Brixham.

Harry Davie had been at sea since 1902, had survived from *Verona* (BM 43), sunk by German U-boat; and on a later occasion had himself rescued the crew of another U-boat victim. He re-registered *Fiery Cross* as BM 145, signed on Bob Soaper as her mate, and worked the English Channel fishing grounds in her for 10 years. '*Fiery Cross* was a nice boat', he told us, 'but beamier than the Brixham-built trawlers, and she had a round stern'. In 1933 he bought the 'mule' class trawler *Girl Inez* and transferred to her the sails, capstan and fishing gear from *Fiery Cross* which was laid up for sale 'as is'. Harry Davie left her in the charge of fish-salesman Charlie Scott, with instructions to accept 'the best offer over £30'. She was eventually sold for a houseboat and so used until February 1937 when the records show that she was sold for breaking. Meanwhile Harry Davie took the *Girl Inez* to the 1935 King's Review at Spithead to represent the Brixham trawler fleet. At the outbreak of World War II, *Fiery Cross* was in Dittisham Creek, and still afloat, having somehow eluded the breakers. By the end of the war she had become entirely derelict and tidal, and it is said that dealers in simulated antique furniture helped themselves to much of her timber.

Official number: 119391. Tonnage: 38·49 gross, 21·77 net. Length: 62·3ft × beam 17·6ft × depth 8·35ft. Ketch rig.

Coal Hulk

Walking the shore of the creek from *Fiery Cross* to the next hulk the would-be marine archaeologist will twice encounter wreckage in the water. These are the sundered parts of a coal hulk; a teak-on-steel purpose-built barge used at Dartmouth when the port was a busy coaling station. She was not engined. Eventually bought by Dittisham men for her valuable timber, she was stripped here in the creek. Hardly a romantic find, but possibly the last evidence of an important period in Dartmouth's history.

In the bight of the creek at SX 859553 can be seen the rudder of the Plymouth ketch-rigged barge *Shortest Day*, propped against the retaining walls of the gardens. Still well-remembered in Plymouth, the *Shortest Day* (c 75 tons) was owned there by Ellis & Rickard; and skippered for years by Capt Honkins, worked chiefly to Falmouth with stone or grain cargoes. We could not discover when she was sold to Dartmouth; but when time-expired she was abandoned on this beach, a cause of much dissatisfaction to the residents who kept boats here. Eventually she was set on fire and burnt out. Her last skipper was Peter Floyd, now deceased.

'The Ship with a Squint' SX 860555

On the village side of Dittisham creek, and opposite the Blackness Rock, is a large wooden hulk only exposed at low water springs, except for some gaunt ribs, which are a favourite resort of the local gulls. Her original name, when a seagoing vessel, remains a mystery; but she may well have been *Esther*, a topsail schooner of the Westcott fleet at Plymouth which was hulked at the end of the Great War and is thought to have been converted to a houseboat.

In palmier days this hulk had been a well-appointed houseboat on the River Yealm when, in the late spring of 1931, she was acquired by the late Joe Tapley, the proprietor of the Totnes cinema. In the July, towage was arranged from the Yealm to the Dart. Mrs Tapley was very concerned because the appointed day was a Friday, reputedly an unlucky day for putting to sea. However, the tow was safely completed, and the white-hulled vessel was moored near the Anchor-Stone. Next day Mr Tapley took his wife to see the vessel, which was beautifully fitted up. There was a large lounge, spacious fully-equipped kitchen, and cabins to sleep ten; moreover the vessel was very well furnished. But Mrs Tapley was appalled. She had been looking earnestly at the female bust figurehead as the boat brought her alongside, and observed that the eyes had a squint! 'No good will come of this', she told her husband. 'You sailed her on a Friday, and she has a cross-eyed figurehead. All we shall get from this ship is bad luck'.

Her words were prophetic. Within 24 hours of returning home Mrs Tapley had a stroke, and never recovered sufficiently to see the ship again before her death some months afterward. Later, thieves boarded the vessel and stole valuable fittings which were never recovered. Eventually, her end came in a gale when she parted her moorings and drove ashore here in Dittisham Creek, becoming a wreck. But the fates had not finished with her owner, who narrowly escaped drowning when his cabin-cruiser *Argyle* was sunk. Not long after, the Totnes Cinema was burned down. Mr Tapley was now elderly and did not long outlive these misfortunes. In accordance with his wishes, his ashes after cremation were placed in two urns. One was interred in his wife's grave, and the other was taken by friends in a boat and dropped in the waters of the Dart he had loved so well. Mrs Florence Prout of Abbotskerswell, who was among the first visitors to the houseboat, believes Joe Tapley had named her *Irene*.

It is probable, though not proven, that *Irene* was the former schooner *Esther*.

Official number: 17069. Built: Shaldon 1856. Tonnage: 98·84 gross, 79·43 net. Length: 80·2ft × beam 19ft × depth 10ft.

Ketch *Winifred*   SX 871527

The *Winifred* was only a small ketch of 38 tons, and her charred remains are gaunt rather than photogenic; but she lies in a tree-shaded, picturesque cove, and the footpath which leads here from Old Mill Lane is a very pleasant walk, especially among the violets and primroses of springtime. This path is followed for several hundred yards 'till it divides, when the lower track is taken down to the cove. A brook and a stile have to be negotiated at the bottom.

Winifred lies among fallen tree branches which the tides have deposited around her. The wreck is much broken up, and has seen a fire aboard; bow and stern have largely gone, but the bilge is virtually complete for the full length of the keel. Portions of the ship's sides still stand, though all the beams are missing. On the port side amidships a fragment of main deck still supports a freshwater tank. On our last visit, the *Winifred* had a more prosperous neighbour; an ex-Naval launch-houseboat was moored immediately astern of her.

Built at Falmouth in 1897, this trim little ketch, of whose early years little is known, was presumably engaged in general trading. Her owner in 1911 is recorded as James Dorey of Lostwithiel. Having survived the Great War, she was sold about 1920 to Captain Purches, an experienced master mariner in coastal craft, who fitted her with her first auxiliary motor. By the 1930s she was owned and skippered by Fred Bowden of Cattedown, Plymouth, with Tom Davey as the mate. In these early days she mostly traded up-channel to Fareham and Portsmouth.

During World War II, she was employed on Government service, delivering gas bottles to the balloon barrage vessels in Falmouth harbour. She changed hands again, at the end of hostilities. Information about her post-war history is as scarce as it is of her early years, except that it is known she spent some years in Brixham harbour during the 1950s. She may have come to Old Mill Creek as a houseboat, or have been towed there for breaking by Distin's of Dartmouth. Photographs of the *Winifred* are rare, but a view of her foredeck is shown on page 147 of Basil Greenhill's *The Merchant Schooners*, volume 2.

Official number: 108553. Registered tonnage: 38.

Walking beyond the *Winifred* around the north shore of the creek – only to be attempted on a falling tide – the anonymous keels of many old vessels will be seen. Two remains are sufficiently substantial to claim our attention.

Unknown steamer   SX 873526

Covered every high tide is the dismembered hulk of a small iron steamer. A pile of twisted ironwork alongside appears to have been the frame of a paddle sponson. It is believed locally that this steamer was abandoned here after 'twilight' service as a fever hulk. Leaving this old paddler, make your way past a fallen tree and the collapsed hull of the trawler *Six Brothers* shows up starkly 50 yards ahead, close to two derelict, steel, ship's lifeboats.

Six Brothers   SX 873526

The *Six Brothers*, built at Jackman's Breakwater Yard, Brixham, in 1897 was a 'mule' class trawler which carried the portmark DH 441 until re-registered in 1902 as BM 144. She was fishing until September 16 1929 when she was dismantled for a hulk and moored here in the Dart, with 'legs' for low water. Private craft often used her as a landing jetty or tie-up berth. The late Lieut Cdr JF Bewley RNR (former captain of P & A Campbell's *Devonia*) considered buying her for conversion to a yacht: but an inspection decided him that her timbers were too ripe. She was partly cut up in 1967 during a spate of river clearance.

Official number: 109291. Tonnage: 48·57 gross, 40·14 net. Length: 67·2ft × beam 18·0ft × depth 8·6ft.

Schooner *Invermore*   SX 874527

During the 1960s passengers on the River Dart excursion boats were constantly asking the crews 'What's the windjammer over there?' Their attention had been arrested, as the steamer passed Old Mill Creek, by the tall masts and spars of the *Invermore*. Today the *Invermore* is still there, on the mud off Rough Point, but her masts, spars and wheelhouse have gone, she fills at every tide, and is a total wreck. Such is the fate of what is claimed to be the last wooden trading schooner built in the British Isles.

Built by J Tyrrell & Sons, of Arklow, Ireland in 1921 of native oak and larch, the *Invermore* with her sister-ship *J T & S* was owned and operated by Tyrrell's (a firm still in existence) for the 36 years of her working life. Registered in Dublin, and based on Arklow, she plied with mixed cargoes in the Home Trade as a three-masted auxiliary schooner. Her name is a corruption of 'In-bhear mor', the Gaelic name for the port of Arklow. Sturdily built for taking the ground in shallow harbours, the *Invermore* has 'no-nonsense' lines, her cruiser style stern giving her a functional but unpretentious silhouette. The design (sometimes called an Irish Sea Stern) gave greater buoyancy aft in following seas and marginally increased accommodation space aft, but was not conducive to fast sailing nor to handy steering as the ship dragged water under the stern. *Invermore* however was designed as an auxiliary schooner, being fitted with a Widdop 2-cylinder oil engine, giving 100hp at 350rpm, and when launched was considered highly-powered. A more powerful motor was fitted in 1938, and her gaff mains'l and mizzen were replaced by jib-headed sails.

In 1957 she was withdrawn from service, and sold in 1960. Shortly after, she was acquired for an emigrant venture from Dartmouth to Australia, taking paying passen-

Forlorn bows of the Invermore, *aground in Old Mill Creek.* Ambrose Greenway.

The auxiliary schooner Invermore *approaches Cumberland basin, Bristol, date unknown.* AJ Edwardes.

gers. Funds failed and the scheme fell through: the ship was left open and exposed to the weather. In 1965, her harbour dues unpaid, the authorities towed her on to the Rough Point mudflats. Thieves stole her helm and some engine parts, and later her spars mysteriously disappeared. The National Maritime Museum has salvaged her Widdop engine, and little of value now remains except her anchor-chains.

By hiring an outboard-motor boat from Dartmouth Quay it is possible at high water to sail right round her or make fast alongside but it is not wise to dally once the tide begins to fall.

Official number: 144972. Tonnage: 146 gross, 78 net.
Length: 92·0ft × beam 22·4ft × moulded depth 11·0ft.
Engined by E Widdop & Co Ltd.

SS *Dartmouth Castle* SX 863522

Dartmouth Castle was the second steamer of that name built for the River Dart Steamboat Company, and was the oldest of the last quartet of steam paddlers which operated

SS Dartmouth Castle, *the sad remains in 1988.* Edwina Small.

for the 15 years prior to World War II. Built of steel in 1907 by Cox & Co of Falmouth, she replaced another paddle steamer of the same name, and was powered by her builders with 2-cylinder compound engines, driving fixed float wheels.

Dartmouth Castle was distinguishable from *Compton Castle*, *Totnes Castle* and *Kingswear Castle* by her narrower deck, not carried out over the sponsons, and her less substantial wheelhouse. Her passenger capacity was less, but she was probably the fastest boat of the four. Strangely, she seems to have largely eluded the photographers: the other steamers feature in many book illustrations and local postcards, but photographs of *Dartmouth Castle* are rare indeed.

When the river service was resumed after the last war, the *Dartmouth Castle* was deemed time-expired. In 1947 she was stripped to the main deck, her engines were lifted out, and she was relegated to a landing stage, at her owner's refitting yard in Old Mill Creek. Hard aground, ballasted and half-covered with soil and gravel, she lies there to this day, grass growing from her decks: but her paddle-wheels are still in position, and her name on the port bow is still discernible.

For those interested in ship construction, and for precision modellers, the *Dartmouth Castle* today presents what is probably a unique opportunity of studying a paddle-wheel at close quarters; for her paddle-boxes have been removed, and the port paddle, still with some floats in position, is exposed to view. But the yard where she lies is private, and permission to view is necessary.

Tonnage: 71 gross, 45 net. Length: 100·4ft × beam 14·6ft × moulded depth 5·3ft.

Ketch *Mizpah* SX 865523

The hulk of this ketch is reached by a footpath through woods. The path leads from a stile at the first bend going down Old Mill Lane, Dartmouth, and brings you to a small promontory crowned by a folly – a small round tower. From here you can look down to the *Mizpah*'s deck a few feet below. She lies port side to the bank, and a waterlogged barge is secured to her starb'd side. At low water it is possible to reach the shore via spiral stairs in the folly, but except for the most agile a ladder is needed to reach her.

The *Mizpah* was launched at Kingsbridge two years before the turn of the century by Date's, for JN Roose & Son of Plymouth. The Rooses, father and son held 32 shares each, bought under mortgage from the Date family. Rather strangely, Roose & Son built another *Mizpah* – a smack-rigged barge of 24 tons – four years later, and for some years appear to have been operating two ships with the same name!

Awaiting the caress of the incoming tide – the ketch Mizpah *at Old Mill Creek.* Martin Langley.

To further complicate research, there were two other vessels of this name periodically in West Country waters at the beginning of the century – a 57-ton Jersey-built ketch, and a Thames barge.

As a member of the Plymouth Roose fleet the *Mizpah* was engaged in general trading until she came into the ownership of the Langmead family of Galmpton. The Haldon pier of Torquay harbour was under construction when the Langmeads secured a contract for delivery of sand and gravel from the Dart to Torquay, before lorry transport. The *Mizpah* and the *Effort* were fitted up as sand barges by Langmeads and auxiliary engines were installed.

It is probable, though not proven, that the *Mizpah* was a balloon-barrage vessel in the Dart in World War II. At the end of the war she was put ashore below the folly in Old Mill Creek, and soon became tidal. It is doubtful if anyone living in the area today knows the hulk's identity, but it should not be thought that the *Mizpah* is mouldering into oblivion. In Gallery 13 of the National Maritime Museum is a display on this ketch in the form of a dioramic reconstruction of her foredeck, and incorporating her pump windlass which was recovered from the hulk, probably not without difficulty, some years ago.

Official number: 108556. Tonnage: 54 gross, 33 net. Length: 68·4ft × beam 18·7ft × 7·1ft. Auxiliary engine 52bhp.

Trawler *Vigilance*

The *Vigilance*, former Brixham trawler BM 76, has her own special place in West Country shipping history: built in 1928, she was the last big ketch-rigged 'sloop' class trawler built by Upham's of Brixham. She has a graceful counter stern, a long run, and skeg at the heel of her keel, over which the rudder turns – a typical product of Upham's yard. Hull, boat and spars cost £1,000.

She was owned by the Foster Brothers, and skippered by George Foster. By 1928 however the Brixham trawl fishery was already in decline: landings of fish – 84,498cwt in 1920 (value £186,920) – had fallen to 43,310cwt in 1928 (value £77,585). Moreover constant losses of gear due to the numerous wartime wrecks sunk on the fishing grounds were a serious matter, for insurance on trawls and warps could no longer be obtained. It was loss of uninsured gear that finally drove the Fosters from business, and the *Vigilance* ceased fishing in 1938, being put up for sale.

It is reasonably certain that during World War II she was used as a naval kite balloon mooring vessel, but not, as far as we can ascertain, in the West Country. Hostilities over, she was sold for conversion to a yacht, being re-registered with Lloyds as a yacht in January 1949, based at Shoreham, Sussex. Her new owner lost his life by drowning when he fell overboard from another yacht; and strangely, on the very night of his cremation, the *Vigilance* was gutted by fire. It may have been coincidence, and the cause of the outbreak was never satisfactorily explained; but it was rumoured that the owner's widow had set fire to the vessel to prevent her sons going to sea. The *Vigilance* was now little better than a wreck, and until 1955 she served as a pontoon and storeroom at Shoreham-by-Sea. She was in this condition when an Australian bought her. Under jury-rig he took her to sea and sailed her 10 miles down channel to Littlehampton, where he had to be towed in by coastguards. It seems he then lost interest, and before 1955 was out had sold *Vigilance* to her present owner, Ken Harris, for £80.

In the spring of 1957 Ken abandoned his job as a shopfitter, and devoted his energies to refitting the ship, whilst living on board. *Vigilance* remained at Littlehampton, and the work of restoration got under way. Initially, Ken Harris replaced what was missing or damaged beyond repair, and generally 'tarted her up'; but being a perfectionist his aims were much higher. Her scars were not easy to hide, and matching old with new was not possible; so during the next 17 years *Vigilance* was rebuilt and replanked upwards from 7 strakes above the keel. Most of the frames were renewed and topsides replanked. Deck beams and deck, deckhouse, skylights and bitts are all new. For these last Ken used a wood called ironbark, obtained from the RN Dockyard. More than 19 tons of oak have gone into new

The restored trawler Vigilance *at Dartmouth Quay*. Herald and Express, Torquay.

frames, deck beams, beam shelf, boards and lodging knees. A ton and a half of iron fastenings, all hand-forged by Ken Harris and then galvanised, have been used for all fastenings. He had to rely on odd jobs for a living and pick up materials and equipment as cheaply as he could. Much outside help was given. One fisherman who was returning to port nearly collided with a large log as it drifted in the river entrance. He reported it to Ken, and before it had drifted too far he had it in tow behind his dinghy and spent the rest of that evening rowing for dear life to get the log ashore!

The lower sections of both masts had been destroyed in the fire. Ken acquired a landing-light post from an aerodrome and scarfed new bottom sections on the main and mizzen masts. The mainmast weighs 2 tons. Its topmast came from a Thames barge. The bowsprit was cut from a pitchpine log chained up at high-water mark near a rubbish dump. It was 50ft long and 15in diameter and was cut down to 40ft × 11in, tapering to 8in. As for canvas, the fores'l and jib were obtained from Hilyard's of Littlehampton, and the mains'l, mizzen and main tops'l were bought secondhand and re-cut. Ken then sailed *Vigilance* to Cowes, where she remained about two years before returning to her home waters in Devon. Restoration is virtually complete, and the ship, based on the Dart, is now available for weekly or daily charter.

It has been a long haul for Ken Harris, but a great achievement.

The *Vigilance*, which cost £1,000 when new, could now be worth nearer £50,000.

Official number: 148999. Tonnage: 39 net.
Length: 78·0ft × beam 19·9ft × depth 8·9ft.

Kingsbridge Estuary

Boats can be hired at Salcombe Quay, where cars can be parked (Pay and display). A boat is the only means of inspecting closely the preserved vessels *Provident*, *Hoshi* and *Egremont* which are moored at a distance from shore. But do not enter the creeks on a falling tide, and use care approaching the tidal wrecks above Tosnos point. These are best visited by driving to Lincombe and obtaining permission to reach the foreshore via Winter's boatyard.

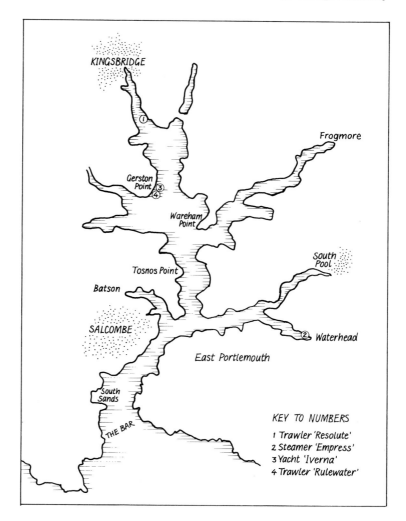

KINGSBRIDGE

Frogmore

Gerston
Point

Wareham
Point

South
Pool

Tosnos Point

Batson

SALCOMBE

Waterhead

East Portlemouth

South
Sands

THE BAR

KEY TO NUMBERS

1 Trawler 'Resolute'
2 Steamer 'Empress'
3 Yacht 'Iverna'
4 Trawler 'Rulewater'

Kingsbridge Estuary
(East Bank)

Trawler *Resolute*   SX 739431

Looking at the pathetic remains of this Brixham trawler today, all one's powers of imagination are needed to picture her in her heyday, standing out of Torbay, with all her russet sails set, and skipper Scott at the helm. *Resolute* was built in 1906 by Jackman's, at their original yard on Brixham Breakwater, with the square transom stern which typified all Jackman's designs. BM 261 was her portmark. She survived the hurricane of December 1910 when four trawlers were lost with all hands, and others suffered damage or lost men overboard, in what skipper Jack

The Brixham trawler Resolute *at King's Quay, with her boat in the water.* Author's collection

Sternpost and deadwood. Little else remains of the once-proud Resolute. Martin Langley.

Widger of *Irex* described as 'the hardest blow I have been in'. Her fishing days ended in April 1937, when she was converted for use as a yacht. During World War II, she was used as a mooring vessel in Brixham harbour.

In 1950 she was sold again and made her last voyage, to Kingsbridge, where she lay alongside the quay for several years. About 1958 she was stripped down and beached beside other hulks a little further downstream. There are three hulks at this spot, and the *Resolute* is the northernmost of the group – to the right as one steps onto the beach. Her remains lie parallel to the water's edge, but consist of little more than the tall, heavy sternpost, part of the rudder, and keel and kelson. Frame timbers and bilge planking have nearly all disappeared. Access is easy, as this is a fairly hard beach, and close to the A 379 road.

Official no: 122893. Tonnage: 48·48 gross, 38·03 net. Length: 66·6ft × 18·6ft × depth 8·35ft. Auxiliary motor fitted in 1931.

Steamer *Empress*   SX 768388

The excursion paddle steamer *Empress* was the third largest of the Saltash, Three Towns & District Steamboat Company's fleet at Plymouth. An iron vessel of 101 tons, she was built by Allsup's of Preston in 1880. A promenade deck extended three-quarters of her length, her funnel was abaft the paddles, and she carried two lifeboats.

There was tragedy on one of her trips up the Tamar. The 'Empress' was turning 'short round' at Weir Head when the son of her master Captain Whitburn lost his balance as

Empress *today in waterhead Creek. Looking aft across the former engine-room.* Martin Langley.

Paddles thrashing the water, Empress *sets course for the Yealm.* Jack Kingston.

the vessel listed, and fell overboard. He drowned in the turmoil of water from the paddles, and his grief-stricken father afterwards emigrated to New Zealand.

Older folk in the Tamar valley remember *Empress* as the 'Market Boat', plying three times a week between Calstock and North-corner, carrying the produce of the valley to Devonport market. Latterly she ran a regular weekly excursion to the Yealm. After withdrawal from service in October 1926 she lay at a buoy, and was kept for a while in reserve. About 1930 she was sold for conversion to a houseboat – which took her back to the Yealm. Eventually dilapidation caused her abandonment, and disused and near-derelict, she was threatening to sink at her moorings. She was then towed on a spring tide by the Plymouth tug *Boarhound* (Capt S Daymond) to the highest reach of Waterhead Creek, and run ashore. Here the once-proud *Empress* became a rather dangerous playground for local children, whose parents petitioned the local authority for her demolition. But here she can still be seen, cut down to her sternpost and bilges, with the forefoot of her bow severed, and lying on the grass bank nearby.

Official number: 81032. Tonnage: 101 gross, 54 net. Length: 115·0ft × beam 16·2ft × depth 4·9ft. Two-cylinder compound engines, by Allsup's. Cyl diameters: HP 16in, LP 30in. Stroke: 30in, NHP 40. Re-boiled 1889 and 1908.

Until very recently the stark, sundered remains of the Brixham trawler Mary Vane Eddy *(1926, 34 tons net) lay in Westerncombe Boat float, Southpool Creek.* Edwina Small.

Kingsbridge Estuary (West Bank)

Yacht *Iverna* SX 745404

The gaunt skeleton of this once-beautiful yacht dominates the 'Graveyard' above Tosnos Point, where she has now lain for over 10 years. The *Iverna* was built in 1890 by JG Fry a Liverpool naval architect who designed a number of large racing cutters of the late 19th century. She was built to order for the famous Jameson brothers; and sailed by John, while brother David later raced the *Britannia* for the king, Edward VII. On occasions she raced against the royal yacht, but was outclassed.

Her original keel was a staggering 58 tons of lead; it was replaced by 40 tons of concrete when her racing days were over. Her hull was of 2in teak planking above the waterline, with pitchpine below. The accommodation below decks was quite luxurious and included a main saloon 17ft × 14ft. The panelling throughout was hand-carved Bermuda Cedar – now unique as this tree died out some years ago. Standing beside the pillaged wreck today one is moved to quote Phinehas' wife and exclaim 'Ichabod! the glory has departed'. But my recommendation is to follow up a visit to *Iverna* with a meal in the Happy Angler

Ichabod, *the glory has departed (2 Samuel 4⁰),* Iverna *in the ships' graveyard at Tosnos.* Edwina Small.

Full and by. Iverna *in her racing days.* Beken of Cowes.

cafe at Salcombe. Not only is the fare good, but here one can recapture something of *Iverna*'s halcyon days, for the proprietor has on display the yacht's helm wheel, capstan crowns, two carved teak bench-ends, a 6in deck nail, and two photographs of the ship under sail.

After the Jameson days the *Iverna* was sailed by Captain William O'Neill, of Ireland, with an experienced crew from Itchen, Hants. Luke Brothers of Hamble reconditioned her in 1924, and in Lloyd's Register of Yachts for 1933 she is recorded as registered in London and owned by Captain Frank Hilder. Her last owner brought her to Salcombe where she was used as a houseboat till 1975 when she was beached and abandoned. Removal of her valuable teak deck hastened her deterioration. Some of her deck hatches and other fittings are now incorporated in the Dartmouth schooner *Pascual Flores.*

Composite-built cutter with gaff rig. Tonnage: 152 gross, 84·40 net. Length: 108·0ft OA, 98·0ft BP × beam 19·0ft × depth 10·7ft. Sail area: 8157 square feet. Sailmaker: Ratsey & Lapthorn. Signal letters LSJD.

BM 353, Rulewater, *at the graveyard, Kingsbridge Estuary. The metal-framed wreck at the extreme left is the racing yacht* Iverna. *The disintegrated hulk in between is the yawl* Cresta.

Trawler *Rulewater* SX 745403

This once-proud Brixham trawler lies a little south of the *Iverna,* but her hull has now fallen on its starb'd side, and collapsed. *Rulewater* was built by Jackman's of Brixham in 1917, in their later yard next to Upham's, and had a fishing career of about 30 years. Carvel-built, with a typical Jackman's square stern, she was classed as a 'mule', as her tonnage was below 40 gross. Her owner/skipper in the 1920s and '30s was Samuel Partridge, and from 1937–39, Harry Davie.

Late in 1939 she was sold for conversion to a yacht but World War II prevented this taking place, and Olsen's Fisherman's Almanack records her as still fishing in 1941, with her original portmark, BM 353. By 1950 her conversion or rather modification for yachting had taken place, but she swung at her moorings bearing a 'FOR SALE' notice. Her last owner took her to Salcombe to become a houseboat-cum-club, but when her harbour dues ceased to be paid she was moved to her last resting place in the 'graveyard'. Even so, as late as 1978 she was still capable of restoration, could a wealthy patron have been found. Her ship's boat, now engined and kept in immaculate condition, is owned by the engineer of Winter's boatyard, and is a familiar sight in the estuary. For many years *Rulewater*'s 8ft tiller was displayed above the bar in the Victoria Inn, Salcombe, but has now been repossessed by its owner.

Official number: 139418. Tonnage: *c* 33 gross, 25 net.

Yacht *Hoshi*

(Article contributed by her skipper, Jeremy Linn)

The Island Cruising Club's schooner *Hoshi* was built as a dayboat by Camper & Nicholson at Gosport 1908–9, rigged as a gaff schooner. A Scotsman named Oswald had *Hoshi* commissioned in 1908 and her launch took place the following year. She was one of the first sailing yachts to have an auxiliary engine, which has always been a diesel. Before she was laid up for the Second World War she had changed owners six times, one of them being the son of Admiral Beatty of Jutland fame. After the war she was extensively rebuilt and this was funded by selling the lead keel and replacing it with a wooden false keel and internal ballast. At this point the rig was reduced to compensate for the fact that she was now very tender in strong winds. The owner before the ICC was 'Chunky' Duff who used her as a charter yacht, the Club buying her from him in 1952.

Hoshi has always sailed around Britain using Brixham, the Solent, Wales and Scotland as her bases. Under Club ownership she has worked out of Salcombe, sailing to Brittany, northern Spain, the Azores, the Baltic area, southern Ireland and all round the British and Scottish coasts. She is entered for the Tall Ships Race and local old Gaffer races.

Official number: 128406. Tonnage: 50 TM. Length: 86·0ft OA including bowsprit, 72·0ft on deck × 14·0ft beam. Draught 9ft.

Trawler *Provident*

Built 1923–4 at Galmpton shipyard on the Dart, the *Provident* was one of the last Brixham trawlers turned out by Sanders & Co, and probably the last 'mule' class boat to join the Brixham Fleet. 'Mule' was the local term for ketch-rigged fishing boats of under 40 tons. She was registered in January 1924, and carried the portmark BM 28. Her semi-elliptical stern, and the small five-pointed star before and after her name, were hallmarks of a Galmpton-built trawler.

She was built for owner/skipper W Pillar, whose previous trawler, also named *Provident*, but of the larger 'sloop' class, had been sunk by a German U-boat in the Great War. (This earlier *Provident* had previously gained distinction by saving 100 men from the battleship *Formidable*, torpedoed by U-24 in West Bay in 1915). Coming as she did at the twilight of the sail-trawler era, *Provident* (2) was fishing for less than 10 years when she was withdrawn and put up for sale.

The Provident *at Salcombe, photographed from the harbourmaster's launch.* Martin Langley.

On 5 January 1933 she was sold to the USA as a yacht. Later she recrossed the Atlantic and was bought by the Island Cruising Club, Salcombe. The Maritime Trust, who wished to preserve a Brixham trawler, then offered to acquire and restore her, and charter her back to the Club. This offer was accepted and the green-hulled *Provident* has since been a familiar sight in the Kingsbridge estuary, cruising during the summer in the western half of the English Channel, with occasional crossings to France. Her appearance has been little altered, except for a midships deckhouse giving access to the accommodation built into the former fish-hold. She has a diesel auxiliary engine, but still carries full trawler rig, including the 'reaching fores'l' favoured by Brixham smacks. She accommodates a crew of 16, having nine saloon berths, three double cabins, and one single cabin.

In 1978 she was torn from her moorings in a spring gale, and came into collision with another vessel, but the damage – to her bulwarks – was slight. In 1985 she was temporarily withdrawn from service pending a major overhaul which has yet to be undertaken.

Official number: 139433. Tonnage: 39·07 gross, 27·19 net. Length: 63·0ft × beam 18·0ft × depth 8·0ft.

M/V *Egremont*

This former Mersey Ferry is now the headquarters of the Island Cruising Club, Salcombe, who would certainly grant permission to visit the vessel to anyone genuinely interested. She is moored in that part of Kingsbridge Estuary known locally as 'The Bag', opposite Tosnos Point. Here she provides a base for the club's cruising fleet and sailing dinghies, cabin accommodation for yachtsmen, a dining room, seamanship and lecture rooms.

The *Egremont*, named after one of the calling places on the Mersey Ferry service, was built as a twin-screw motor vessel by Philip's of Dartmouth in 1952. She was a sister-ship to the M/V *Leasowe II*, completed a year earlier. One thousand four hundred and seventy two passengers could be carried on the Seacombe-Liverpool run, and 700 when river cruising. There was a saloon (convertible to a ball-room) on the main deck, and a buffet, bar, and smokeroom on the lower deck. The propelling machinery (now removed) consisted of two 8-cylinder Crossley Diesel engines of the direct-reversible 2-stroke type, with a bhp of 1280.

The Island Cruising Club purchased *Egremont* in 1976. She was dry-docked at Birkenhead for survey, hull preservation and removal of shafts, propellers and rudders, after which her engines were dismantled. The tug *Sea Bristolian* towed her from Birkenhead to Salcome, where she arrived after a 72-hour trip on 18 June 1976. Since then a great deal of work has been carried out to convert her to a club headquarters, aided for four months in 1977 by workers of a Job Creation programme. Externally the most noticeable change is the disappearance of lifeboats and davits from the boat deck, making way for a large deckhouse of cabins abaft the funnel.

Tonnage: 566 gross. Length: 147·0ft OA, 138·7 BP × beam 34·1ft × depth 11·3ft. Engined by Crossley Bros of Manchester.

Hen and chicks. The Egremont *with keelboats and dinghies around her.* Island Cruising Club.

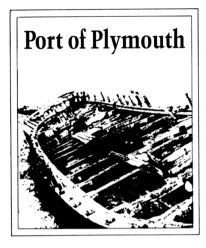

Port of Plymouth

River Plym

Apart from the *Antelope* in the Laira, and the unidentified small steamer by the Passage House Inn, all the hulks are in Hooe Lake. To reach the Radford end of the lake, cross Laira Bridge, turn right into Oreston Road, left into Plymstock Road, then right (beside disused railway) and down to the gatehouse known locally as 'the Castle'. Park here, by the waterside.

To reach the Cattewater end of the lake, take the Pomphlett road after crossing Laira Bridge, turn right into Dean Cross Road, follow it through into Radford Park Road, turn right into Hooe Road, and park at Hooe Quay.

Motor boats can only be hired at a distance – from West Hoe Basin. Do not enter Hooe Lake on a falling tide.

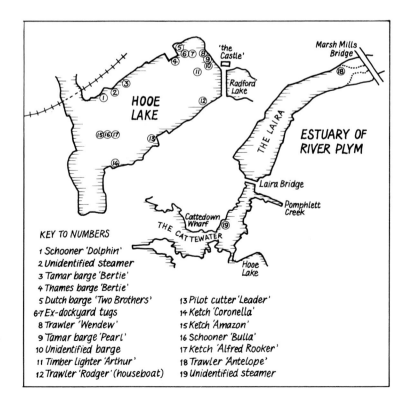

KEY TO NUMBERS

1 Schooner 'Dolphin'
2 Unidentified steamer
3 Tamar barge 'Bertie'
4 Thames barge 'Bertie'
5 Dutch barge 'Two Brothers'
6-7 Ex-dockyard tugs
8 Trawler 'Wendew'
9 Tamar barge 'Pearl'
10 Unidentified barge
11 Timber lighter 'Arthur'
12 Trawler 'Rodger' (houseboat)
13 Pilot cutter 'Leader'
14 Ketch 'Coronella'
15 Ketch 'Amazon'
16 Schooner 'Bulla'
17 Ketch 'Alfred Rooker'
18 Trawler 'Antelope'
19 Unidentified steamer

River Plym (West Bank)

Trawler *Antelope* SX 512560

The dismasted hull of the *Antelope* has long been a familiar but probably anonymous sight to thousands of motorists entering or leaving Plymouth by the A38 on the Laira Embankment; for she lies in a conspicuous position just off the railway carriage-siding.

Originally a Brixham trawler of the 'sloop' class, the *Antelope* was built by Robert Jackman of Brixham in 1906, and for 10 years fished from that port under the registration BN 128. On March 26, 1916, her owner-skipper, Francis Bond, sold her to Plymouth, having replaced her by a newer trawler, the *Seaplane*.

At Plymouth *Antelope* was re-registered as PH 94, and whilst still engaged in trawling, became a fishery protection vessel. The RN Dockyard fitted an auxiliary engine and mounted a gun on her foredeck. Two Naval gunnery ratings supplemented her crew for the duration of the Great War. Her owner-skipper was Charlie Drake, whose son (of the same name) served as a third hand; Bill Hill was the mate. In the late 1920s she was owned by 'Jonny' Taylor, famed locally as skipper of the *Erycina*. When steam trawlers finally ousted the smacks from the English Channel fishing grounds in the 1930s, the *Antelope* was laid up. Her World War II service is not known but it is probable that she became a balloon-barrage vessel. The war over, she was sold for conversion to a yacht, and last appeared in Lloyd's Register of Yachts in 1952. Eventually she was acquired by two partners, who in or about 1962 brought her to her present position, stripped her of all marketable fittings and abandoned her.

There is no access to the wreck by land: but she may be reached by boat during the last hour of a flooding tide, when there is sufficient water on her star'd side to draw alongside. Even in her dereliction, she bears evidence to the craftsmanship of Jackman's shipyard.

Official number: 122885. Tonnage: 49·97 gross, 39·08 net. Length: 67·3ft × beam 18·2ft × moulded depth 8·65ft. Carvel built, transom stern, ketch rig.

Unidentified small steamer SX 494535

The sturdy remains of what appears to have been a small steamer *c* 40ft in length lie on the river beach, outside Passage House Inn, by Cattedown Wharves. All attempts at identification have failed. A few yards to the west are slight remains exposed at low water, and covered in weed, of the former Turnchapel steam ferry *Swift*.

Built to last by Jackman's: the trawler Antelope *yields slowly to time on the Laira.* Edwina Small.

River Plym
(East bank, Hooe Lake)

Amazon, Bulla, Alfred Rooker   SX 498527

The visitor to Hooe Lake will immediately notice, offshore from Hooe Quay, the prominent sternpost of a derelict wooden vessel, projecting sheer from the water. If the tide is low, the entire keel and kelson will be exposed; for the wreck dries out before low water. Almost certainly there will be a 'watch on deck', as gulls and cormorants are invariably in occupation. The cloying mud around the remains makes approach difficult: and those who do not enjoy the fun of trying to lift their feet without losing their 'wellies' are advised to use an inflatable dinghy and time arrival for just before the wreck is washed by a rising tide. Most may well consider the reward not worth the effort, but the aspiring marine archaeologist will perhaps relish the challenge, for here are, in fact, the remains of three vessels, and the identity of one is uncertain. After numerous discussions with ancient mariners of Hooe and Oreston in the King's Arms, we are satisfied that the prominent sternpost and its keel are the remains of the ketch *Amazon*. As for the jumbled remains alongside, they certainly include what is left of the Barnstaple schooner *Bulla* and probably the Plymouth ketch *Alfred Rooker*.

Ketch *Amazon* Built by Le Soeur of Jersey in 1966 *Amazon* was first registered at Hull. She was lengthened in 1870/1 and if, as believed, the measurements given here relate to after lengthening, she probably started life as a trawler, working on the East Coast. From 1900 until the outbreak of the Great War – and perhaps later – her master was AJ Watts. In 1904 she was registered at Barnstaple for Bessie, wife of James Watts, master mariner of Braunton. We have been unable to establish whether she had come west from Hull in 1900, as seems probable; nor whether, as also seems likely, AJ Watts and James Watts were related – or identical.

In 1927 she was sold to Oscar Harris, mariner of Par, who re-registered her at Barnstaple and installed an auxiliary motor of 25bhp. Her new owner/skipper was something of a character. Jack Birch of Oreston recalls that he was nick-named 'Mad' Harris on account of his uncertain temper 'when things were not going right!' He was a native of Par and his mate was likewise a Cornishman. In the late '20s and early '30s the *Amazon* was probably better known for her colourful skipper than for any other reason. But that was to change when she acquired a jinx in 1934.

On June 16 that year she caught fire in the engine-room when off Looe. She came to anchor off Whitepatch and her

Amazon *at Hooe Lake, showing ex-pilot cutter* Leader *as houseboat in the background.* Martin Langley.

crew succeeded in quelling the fire with seawater after two desperate hours. No doubt 'Mad' Harris's uncertain temper was greatly excercised during this time! Then, continuing her voyage, *Amazon* reached Plymouth and berthed in Millbay Docks to offload her cargo of maize. That night however the fire flared up again, in the hold, and fire-engines were summoned to deal with it. Her cargo was discharged, repairs were carried out, and the *Amazon* sailed again.

But her jinx had not forsaken her. Two years later, on September 22, 1936, she stranded whilst entering Plymouth, and strained her hull badly, near Picklecombe Fort. Her crew took to the boat, and were escorted into harbour by the Plymouth lifeboat. The *Amazon* was later brought in by a tug, surveyed, and found to be beyond economic repair. Written off as a total loss, she was towed into Hooe Lake and left to rot. One of her masts was acquired by Rogers Shipyard, Cremyll, who constructed a boat from it.

Official number: 55260. Tonnage: 49 gross, 34 net.
Length: 65·5ft × beam 17·4ft × depth 8·2ft.

Schooner *Bulla* This was a two-masted tops'l schooner built at Deslandes, Jersey, 1873, and registered at Barnstaple. By 1902 she was owned and managed by Ernest Brown of Port Isaac, and after World War I was based at Plymouth but owned by John Marwood of Liverpool. In her last years of trading her owner was John H Davies of Plymouth, and the names of her skipper and mate were Rice and Hine respectively. In January 1928 her registry was closed with the entry 'converted to a lighter'; and within a few years, probably spent timber-carrying for Bayly's, she was abandoned here in Hooe Lake.

Official number: 68755. Tonnage: 87 gross, 75 net.

Ketch *Alfred Rooker* A product of Darton of Plymouth in 1876, the *Alfred Rooker* was named to commemorate a 19th century Plymouth alderman, who had been Mayor from 1873–4. The ketch was originally employed in the Corunna cattle trade, between Spain and Bullocks' Dock in the Hamoaze, and is said to have made the record passage for the cattlemen. She was then transferred to the Newfoundland Cod trade, which was at its peak between 1890 and 1910. In 1909 her owner is recorded as Henry Holton of Oreston. The Newfoundland trade, in which some British vessels continued until the 1930s, was much diminished after the Great War, and by then the *Alfred Rooker* had been relegated to coasting. In the post-war years she was one of Davis & Stephens (Plymouth) fleet, and her owner/manager was WK Stephens of Wolster Street. During her latter years she was skippered by AJ

Brown, the mate's name being Weare. In 1934, after 58 years of strenuous working life, she was dismasted at Cattedown and tied alongside the *Bulla*, to rot quietly away.

Official number: 68350. Tonnage: 76 gross, 59 net.
Length: 71·6ft × beam 19·5ft × depth 9·2ft.

Cutter *Leader* SX 499527

Formerly a well-known Plymouth pilot cutter, the *Leader*, after 58 years as a houseboat, is today a broken hulk in process of being cut up – a sad end to a historic vessel.

A fleet of privately owned pilot cutters operated from Plymouth in the days of sail. Early boats resembled fishing smacks but gradually lines were made finer in the quest for speed. Even so, the cutters had to be good seaboats, able to patrol the often turbulent waters of the English Channel in all weathers. The *Leader* designed and built by H Grigg of Plymouth in 1867, represented the final development and was the fastest cutter on the Plymouth station, especially to windward, and probably anywhere in the south west.

Owned and skippered by senior pilot JA Glinn, the *Leader* remained in service well into the present century. She was sold for conversion to a houseboat in 1926. Later

The Plymouth pilot cutter Leader *showing her paces. She was renowned for speed and sailing qualities.* AJ Glinn.

she suffered a mishap, falling on to her beam during an ebb tide, but her sturdy hull enabled her to survive, none the worse. Nemesis overtook this once fleet and handsome craft in December 1984, when her mooring arrangements were not proof against a high tide whipped up by gale force winds, and she was swamped. The leg on her starb'd side collapsed under the weight of the flooded vessel as the tide fell, and the *Leader*'s fate was sealed. This was a tragedy, for *Leader* was an important part of Plymouth's maritime heritage, and there were those who hoped that she might one day be restored, and displayed in her former glory.

Official number: 56664. Tonnage: 34·56 net.
Length: 67·5ft × beam 15·3ft × depth 9·2ft.

Also in Hooe Lake

Houseboat *Roger*   SX 503528

The former Belgian trawler, now serving as a houseboat, is moored in the shade of the trees on the south bank. A small steel-built motor trawler, she was built at Nieuport in 1947 and sold to Brixham in 1966. She fished out of Brixham with the portmark BM 172 under an owner/skipper named Ribbie, until sold to a Plymouth fisherman in May 1974. Some months later she was bought by a yachtsman intending to base her in Scotland for long-distance cruising. Additional fuel tanks were built into her by Mashford's of Cremyll, who, when instructions for further alterations proved not forthcoming and her dues remained unpaid, sold her for conversion to a houseboat.

No official number (not registered under Part I, Merchant Shipping Act). Tonnage: 27·23 gross and net. Length: 60·5ft OA, 51·5ft BP × beam 17·4ft × depth in hold 6·5ft.

Barge *Arthur*   SX 503530

Conspicuous at the east end of the lake, and lying just offshore, is the almost complete framework of a large lighter, from which much of the hull planking has been removed. This is the *Arthur*, a dumb barge formerly owned by Bayly's the timber importers. She did her work in tow of Bayly's small steam tug *Alice*, whose fate is unknown.

Thames barge *Bertie* SX 50253

This Thames sprits'l barge, now fast disintegrating, was built at Faversham in 1901 and originally used in the brick trade. Eventually, proving too small for economic trading, she came west to the Kingsbridge Estuary where she served as a barge-yacht, until becoming unseaworthy. She was then towed to Plymouth for conversion to a house-boat. Her present owner, Fred Easton, bought her in 1970 and removed her mast and lee-boards. Her mainmast head, with topmast bracket and crosstrees still attached, lies on the south shore, with both leeboards close by. The hull has long been tidal.

Official number: 104948. Tonnage: 55 gross, 43 net, 105 deadweight. Length: 77·5ft × beam 17·8ft × depth in hold 5·01ft.

Remains of three vessels SX 504530

The keels and slender remains of three vessels can be seen, side by side, on the east shore, near the 'castle'. Formerly three hulls moored alongside each other and floating every high tide, they gradually fell into this decay. They are, from left to right: an unidentified craft with both stem and sternpost standing; the *Pearl*, a Tamar sailing barge once busy in the stone trade and based at Saltash Passage; and the *Wendew*, a 'mule' class Brixham trawler (BM 119) which came to Plymouth in 1940. Her former owner/skipper, Dan Friend, has a fine painting of *Wendew* under sail, in his Brixham home. Eddie Blackler, her last owner, made her his houseboat-home for several years.

Pearl Official number: 132759. Built: 1840. Tonnage: 50 burthen, 24·3 net.
Wendew Official number: 139411. Built: 1912. Tonnage: 35·16 gross, 24·15 net. Length: 62·2ft × beam 15·7ft × depth 7·7ft.

New lease of life. Bateau *at Hooe Lake*. B Butcher.

Yacht *Bateau* (Afloat and at work)

Despite her French name, this trim little yacht was built in Falmouth, in 1910 by WE Thomas. She is constructed of pine on oak, with carvel planking and a counter stern, and her original rig was gaff yawl. She was first engined in March 1949 with a 2-cylinder 4hp petrol Brockhouse; and was first registered in 1952, when her owner was company director Frank Wade of Birmingham. In 1956 she was sold to Norman Palmer of Philleigh on the Fal and changed hands again when bought in 1969 by Joseph Fairless off St Austell. A year later another St Austell yachtsman, John Greenaway, had become her owner and in 1973 she was purchased by John Heap of Bodmin. About 1980, in need of overhaul, she was laid up at Fowey and began to deteriorate.

When Barrie Butcher, her present owner, found her in 1984 she was still watertight but in otherwise poor condition. However, he bought her, and had then to wait four months for good enough weather to tow her to Plymouth. The work of restoration then began: a new deck and cockpit, rebuilt cabin top, mast reset 6ft aft and shortened by 3ft. She has been re-rigged as a Bermudan cutter, and on trial in 1986 sailed 'like a gem'. She is based in Hooe Lake.

Length: 25ft 0in × beam 7ft 4in. Draught: 4ft 6in.
Length BP: 20ft 3½in. Registered tonnage: 2·76.

Breton Tunnyman *Petite Marie Claude*
(Afloat and at work)

This former fishing vessel built in 1964 is scarcely a veteran but has ended one phase of life to begin another. For 16 years she fished for tunny in the Bay of Biscay and 'carried the scars of her service in those unforgiving waters'. She entered the port of Douarnenez for the last time in August 1980 with her future uncertain. There she was laid up, stripped of working gear and apparently left to rot.

Ted Littlejohn, an Anglican clergyman working amongst the young unemployed in Walsall, heard of *Petite Marie Claude* and felt she could fulfil a dream. In December 1985 he acquired her for his organisation Workability Plus which for some years had been taking parties of young unemployed to Dartmoor for Outward Bound type holidays – camping, hiking, canoeing and rock-climbing. He wanted to be able to take them to sea.

Petite Marie Claude was brought across the Channel under her own power; and conversion, which began at Exeter canal basin, was completed by Plymouth Community Boatyard in Stonehouse Pool, the work being financed by the Manpower Services Commission. Accommodation was provided for 15 people, and a new rig designed to give her sail power. On Palm Sunday, April 12, 1987, the ship was commissioned by Mrs Shelagh Keyse of the Manpower Services Commission, in the presence of the Lord Mayor. She is now based at Queen Anne's Battery, but with moorings in the Cattewater. Youngsters in the 16–18 age group spend five days aboard at a time learning about life aboard ship and the importance of both team spirit and self-reliance.

Tonnage: 48·25 gross. Length: 60·0ft.

River Tamar

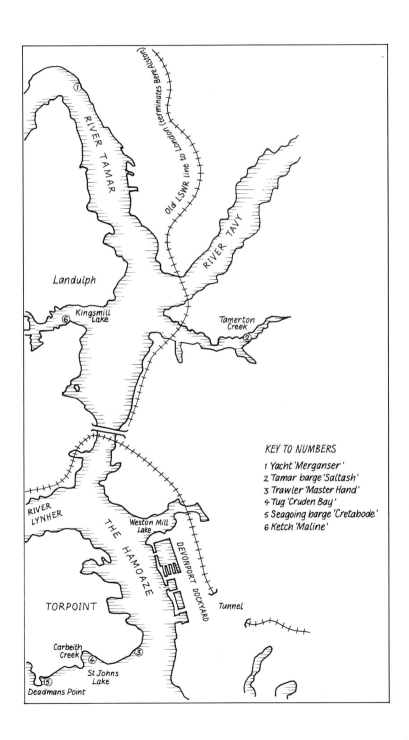

KEY TO NUMBERS

1 Yacht 'Merganser'
2 Tamar barge 'Saltash'
3 Trawler 'Master Hand'
4 Tug 'Cruden Bay'
5 Seagoing barge 'Cretabode'
6 Ketch 'Maline'

Excursion boats up the Tamar (from Phoenix Wharf) will give you a distant view of the *Merganser*, and a fairly close view of the restored *Shamrock* at Cotehele, but no more. Hired boats are not recommended: the distances are considerable, and the Hamoaze is no place for the inexperienced.

By car, take the Tamar Bridge for Cotehele and the *Shamrock*; take the Torpoint Ferry for the *Master Hand*, *Cruden Bay* and *Cretecove*. The *Saltash* lies on the south side of Station Road, Tamerton Foliot, Plymouth, at the foot of a wooded bank.

River Tamar (East Bank)

Yacht *Merganser*   SX 430653

This interesting old vessel with very pleasing lines has been a houseboat, in the same berth, for over 50 years. She can be viewed, close-up, from the road which rises from the bank of Tamar, at Hole's Hole, towards Bere Alstone. *Merganser* is a thoroughbred, designed by Benjamin Nicholson, father of CE Nicholson, a yacht designer of repute: and built by Camper & Nicholsons at Gosport in 1887 – which makes *Merganser* almost a centenarian.

She was built as a cutter-rigged yacht for Hugh Leyborne Popham, of Littlecote, Hungerford, and it was he that brought her down to Plymouth. Ian Merry (author of *The Westcotts and their Times*) believes that *Merganser* came to Plymouth shortly before the Great War, and tells me that her owner then converted her into a fishing smack. Certainly she was registered commercially and given the portmark PH 37. Whether she was able to continue fishing during hostilities or was requisitioned for some special duty I cannot ascertain, but in 1920 she came on to the market.

Samuel Boon Harvey, a Plymouth sailmaker and shipbroker, bought her on February 19 that year, but sold her again four years later. On June 24 1924 she was acquired by Robert Dell, a Commissioned Gunner of the Royal Navy. He beached her on her present mud berth, which was close to his home, and converted her to a houseboat. Nearly six years later she was again 'FOR SALE', and on January 31 1930 was bought by George Charles Evans, a stove and grate merchant of Plymouth. Mr Evans' daughter and her husband lived aboard the *Merganser* for some years. At some time during the '40s she passed to a family named Hall, who made her their home and brought up four sons on board. In July 1952 the Registrar of Shipping closed her entry as 'vessel used only as a houseboat'.

Awaiting her fate. Always reprieved until now, Merganser *faces an uncertain future.* Edwina Small.

The years were taking their toll, and when the Halls moved out *Merganser*'s fate was in the balance. Her stern had suffered distortion, her ballast had been entirely removed, and most of her upper fastenings had been drawn. The Parish Council placed a demolition order on her, and the National Maritime Museum intervened to see if she could be saved. A survey however showed that it would not be safe to move her. It was then that fate, in the form of TV playwright Eric Paice and his wife, Alison, smiled on *Merganser*. After seeing the hulk advertised in *The Times*, they decided she needed care and attention, so bought her and set about restoring her up as far as her gunwhales. They entrusted this formidable, four-year task to the local Charley Hingston, a skilled shipwright. The hull was restored to its original shape, and the main deck cleared of all top hamper. Once again *Merganser* resembled the thoroughbred that she is. By 1986 however Mr Paice had been unable to make his customary holiday use of the ship for some months; and to avert an unwelcome takeover by squatters, a local resident bought the *Merganser* from Mr Paice. As her new owner will not require her as a houseboat, her chances of reaching her hundredth birthday must now be considered less than even. If fate is to smile again on *Merganser*, it must do so very soon indeed.

Official number: 91817. Tonnage: 56 net.
Length: 68·2ft × beam 17·4ft × moulded depth 10·9ft.

Tamar Barge *Saltash* SX 460605

The Tamar barge *Saltash* had a long and useful life of nearly 100 years and was something of a chameleon. Launched in 1864 as the cutter-rigged yacht *Desmond*, she was lengthened in 1891 and then underwent radical alteration by ship-builder John Westcott of Lower Cleave Houses, Bideford, in 1899. Westcott's conversion altered her from 'a sharp keeled yacht to an almost flat-bottomed cargo vessel'. (Grahame Farr's comment in his monograph *Shipbuilding in North Devon*, No 22 176). Renamed *Iron King* and re-rigged as a 43-ton ketch by 1903, she was then registered at Bideford and owned by John Moss of Clovelly. By 1919 she was owned and managed by William Acford of Appledore, and a 30hp auxiliary engine was installed in 1922.

At some time in the mid-'twenties she came to the Tamar, and 'Captain Alf Taylor of Calstock sailed her some years with his son as crew' (Ian Merry in his monograph *Shipping and Trade of the River Tamar* Part II, No 46 1980). By 1929 she had been renamed *Saltash*, and was in the ownership of Jefford & Sons, Ltd, of Burraton Combe, who used her for carrying stone from their quarries. They had a new keel fitted by Goss of Calstock that year. Still ketch-rigged, she is said by Torpoint long-shoremen to have resembled the now-restored *Shamrock*, and like her she made voyages outside the port limits of Plymouth down the south coast of Cornwall. In 1944 she was re-engined, and worked out her remaining years on the Tamar, a familiar sight at Torpoint, Calstock, and intervening quays. In the '50s, considered time-expired, she was sold to the Plymouth Boy Scouts Association and ended her days as a headquarters boat in Tamerton Creek, where her remains can still be seen.

Official number: 91067. Tonnage: 56 gross, 32 net.
Length: 74·4ft × beam 17·6ft × moulded depth 7·1ft.

River Tamar (West Bank)

Trawler *Master Hand*   SX 441549

Survivor of the once huge sail-trawler fleet of Lowestoft, the *Master Hand* was built in 1920 by G & T Smith Ltd, of Rye, Sussex, who were renowned for the standard of their craftsmanship. The cost was £2,400, but in her first three years of fishing, under skipper JT Crouch, her earnings averaged £2,000 per annum for Messrs Breach and Goffin, her owners. Registered with the portmark LT 1203, *Master Hand* fished the North Sea for more than 18 years, until the outbreak of World War II.

Throughout the war she was moored on the Norfolk Broads as an obstruction to enemy seaplanes or flying-boats; but in 1946 she was towed to Ramsgate, overhauled and fitted with an engine. In November of that year she left for Brixham and new owners.

Working from Brixham her first three weeks fishing realised £830. In August 1947 she was re-registered as

Despair replaces hope: the Lowestoft-built Master Hand *at Chapeldown Beach.* Martin Langley.

The launch of Master Hand *at Rye in 1920. Her first skipper, JT Crouch, is standing second from the bow and owned the original of this photograph.*

BM 43. Retired fisherman Ned Widger of Brixham who skippered her told us 'she was a good sea-boat'. But her stay in the port which has been called the 'Mother of the Trawl Industry' was short-lived. By 1949 she had been sold again, and joined the trawl fleet at Plymouth.

Here she retained her Brixham fishing number, and continued trawling until about 1968. Her last skipper was Joseph Frude of Plymouth, who recalls that when she was retired from fishing she was much in need of overhaul and was 'seeping water around the shaft tunnel'.

Mashford Bros, shipbuilders at Cremyll, acquired the *Master Hand* after she was laid up: and with her engine and propellor removed and sold, she lay in their yard until bought by John Blowers, her present owner. She now lies on Chapeldown beach, Torpoint, awaiting intended restoration, which every passing year makes more improbable.

The *Master Hand* has figured prominently in a number of books and publications over the years; and her design and construction (see EJ March's *Sailing Trawlers*) are probably better documented than any other British fishing vessel.

Official number: 14001. Tonnage: 45·75.
Length: BP 70ft × beam 19ft × moulded depth 9ft.

All things come to an end, even the life of a busy tug. Cruden Bay *at Carbeile.* John Cotton.

Tug *Cruden Bay* SX 433548

The remains of the wooden steam tug *Cruden Bay* lie in Carbeile Creek, near the site of the mill. Built by W Jarvis of Anstruther in 1899 as a steam trawler, she was owned and managed by Thomas Davidson of Aberdeen, then her port of registry. In 1912 she came south to work as a tug, and was re-registered at Falmouth that year. We have no record of her World War I service, but by 1919 she was employed at Fowey, under the ownership of Ernest Chaplin of London, but managed locally by Henry Paull. Chaplin sold her in 1920 to the Fowey Tug and Salvage Company, who worked her for about three years, mostly berthing china clay freighters.

She was then purchased by the Port of Plymouth tug owners WJ Reynolds of Torpoint, and the voyage from Fowey to Plymouth proved to be her last. By 1929 she was deregistered, and lay for years unused on Torpoint beach, cannibalized for spares. When she had no more to give, *Cruden Bay* was ignominiously towed to Carbeile Creek and abandoned where her remains lie now. *Cruden Bay* has had the last laugh on the firm that spurned her services for she is the only Reynolds' tug of which there are any remains today.

Official number: 108669. Tonnage: 125 gross, 43 net.
Length: 96·7ft × beam 20·3ft × depth 10·7ft. Engines: 47hp.

Cretabode; an enigma to all who catch sight of her. Edwina Small.

Seagoing Barge *Cretabode* SX 425543

This hulk, whose name is now indecipherable, was for long a mystery to us. She lies beached off Deadman's Point, St John's Lake, on the Cornish side of the estuary, and her hull, which is not unshapely, is of reinforced concrete. She is, in fact, a war-emergency seagoing barge, of which many were built during both world wars, mostly by Mersey or Scottish shipyards. Some were used as mobile grain warehouses, or huge coal lighters. Others, of the 1943 variety, as military stores transports in the invasion of Normandy.

Our hulk has a counter stern, a slight sheer, and is probably about 130ft long by about 22ft beam. Her quadrilateral steel rudder is not unlike those fitted to some diesel coasting tramps. Eventually a letter from Alan Tarr of Ramsey, Isle of Man, identified her as one of the craft built by, or for, Concrete Seacraft Ltd, of which his father was managing director and owner. All had names prefixed by *Crete*, and none were engined. The company's shipyard was at Fidler's Ferry on the Mersey and the barges were constructed between 1918 and 1919. However, there was a subcontractor at Hamworthy, Poole: and it was there that this vessel, the *Cretabode*, was launched in 1918. Although inherently long-lasting, in the event few of the craft had long lives because their size and their reliance on tugs gave them a limited application. One foundered in Morecambe Bay and lay on the seabed for 20 years before an enterprising salvor raised her and put her into service again! In general however, information is scarce; for no one, it seems, ever made it their business to log the careers of these unromantic craft.

The *Cretabode* was laid up with another between the wars in Wiveliscombe Creek. In the 'fifties, Viscount Lennox-Boyd, then Colonial Secretary, acquired Ince Castle and took objection to these hulks in front of his house. The queen's harbourmaster obliged by removing them to the Torpoint foreshore, just west of the ballast pond. This provoked vehement protest from the local inhabitants, so one was towed out to sea and scuttled. The *Cretabode* however had been damaged in beaching, and was only refloated with difficulty. She was then (*c* 1965) towed to her present position and scuttled to inhibit erosion of the shore protecting what is now the rifle-range of HMS *Raleigh*, but was once a graveyard – hence 'Deadman's Point'.

As built, the *Cretabode* had a concrete guard-rail at bow and stern, hatchcombing amidships, and a wheelhouse, funnel, and boat-in-davits aft. The smokestack was from a boiler which served winches, pumps and other auxiliaries. All these superstructures have long gone, cut away by some previous owner who wanted a flat deck area.

If permission is sought to walk the path through the RN officers' golf course at Trevol, it is possible to get opposite the wreck for photographs; but an approach across the muddy strand is not recommended. A boat can circle the hulk, which dries out at low water, once the tide has reached half-flood.

Official number: 142701. Built: 1918. Registered tonnage: 620.

River Tamar (West Bank)

Ketch *Maline*   SX 428608

This old Danish fishing vessel is not easy of access, hiding coyly at Skinham Point on the west bank of Tamar. Built in 1912 at Bornholm as a gaff-rigged ketch, she is a 'double-ender', iron-fastened, with a 1in clinker planking. Her present owner, TW Prosser, was a World War II DEMS gunner, and after converting *Maline* for cruising, sailed her in the Mediterranean, through the French canals, and on many Channel cruises.

She has lain at this secluded spot since 1982, and though there are plans to restore her to her original condition, it will be a considerable task and she looks unlikely to leave her present berth. Her Bolinder engine was replaced by a Mercedes which is now flooded. A small deckhouse has replaced her mizzen mast.

Length: 38·0ft × beam 12·5ft. Tonnage: *c* 14.

River Tamar – The Hamoaze

Eagle & Ark Royal

By far the largest and best-known of all Westcountry hulks left the scene before this book was produced. These were the Royal Navy's last two fleet carriers. HMS *Eagle* lay moored in the Hamoaze for over six years from August 1972 to October 1978 before being towed away for scrap. Her sister-ship *Ark Royal* occupied the mooring vacated by *Eagle*'s departure from summer 1979 to autumn 1980 before making the same last voyage to Cairnryan.

Tamar Barge *Shamrock* (Restored)   SX 423682

The ketch-rigged *Shamrock*, now lying at Cotehele Quay, is the only survivor of the once numerous fleet of sailing barges on the River Tamar. Throughout the 19th century and until the coming of the railway to Calstock in 1908 and the trade repercussions of the Great War, these barges transported all the products of the Tamar Valley. Cargoes of copper, tin, arsenic, silver, lead, coal, manure, domestic briquettes, lime, stone, brick, grain, vegetables and fruit were carried between the Tamar quays and Plymouth; and by the larger vessels to the Bristol Channel, Ireland, and European ports.

The *Shamrock* was built at Hawke's shipyard, Stonehouse, Plymouth, in 1899, for Tom Williams, a Torpoint lighterman, who owned her for 20 years. She was ketch-rigged with pitchpine masts and spars, and flax canvas sails, and designed for work inside the limits of Plymouth Breakwater.

At her first change of ownership, in 1919, structural alterations were made to the hull, a new rudder was provided, and a 30ihp paraffin engine installed. She was then re-classified to carry cargo at sea, beyond the harbour limits, and commenced work in the stone trade, in which she was to be engaged for the next 42 years, under various owners. Her last voyage as an auxiliary sailing vessel was on the Cornish coast in 1962.

In 1963 *Shamrock* was converted to a fully-powered motor ship, with twin-screw diesel engines. She now entered on a third lease of life which was to last seven years, serving first as a salvage dredger at Falmouth, and later as a diving tender at Plymouth.

In 1970 she was hulked and lay semi-derelict in Hooe Lake until purchased by the National Trust in 1974 and towed to a slip at Cotehele Quay. There her restoration proceeded with the assistance of the National Maritime Museum. Five years work followed, undertaken by crafts-

Swansong. Mourners pay their last respects as HMS Eagle *makes her final public appearance, bound for the breakers.* The Press Association.

Restoration in progress on the Tamar sailing barge Shamrock *at Cotehele, February 1977.* Western Morning News.

men George Eley and Tom Perkins and workers of the Manpower Services Commission. She was refloated in 1979, recommissioned on August 15th that year, and has since been on view to the public, restored to her 1920 condition.

Official number: 111344. Tonnage: 31·71 gross and net. Length: 57·6ft × beam 18·1ft × depth 5·4ft.

Smack *JNR*   SX 433647 Weir Quay

The *JNR* is the lone survivor of the numerous sailing smacks which once worked from the Port of Plymouth and traded in the coastal waters. She was built in 1893 by Date of Kingsbridge for the Roose family, shipowners and ship-builders of Plymouth. James Nicholson Roose (hence the name JNR) was her owner/skipper, with his son who rejoi-ced in the same name, as Mate.

This smack had a reputation – shared with Westcott's *The Sirdar* – for being a fast sailer, and it was seldom she was overhauled. William Hobbs of Morwellham, skipper of a rather slow barge *Myrtle*, had to put up with a lot of banter from the 'speed merchants': and *JNR*'s skipper was among those who would wave a rope's end on coming abeam, in mock offering of a tow, or overhaul him as he was nearing a quay and have hatches open before the *Myrtle* had made fast!

Ian Merry in his book *The Westcotts and their Times* (1977) mentions a pensioner then aged 73 and living in Exmouth, who recalled loading brick cargoes on the *JNR* at Cotehele Quay in the early 1920s. The move to mechanisation which swept the coastal fleets in the 'twenties caught up with the *JNR* in 1927, when a 5hp auxiliary engine was installed. The Mercantile Navy list for 1929 records her owner/skipper as William Webber of North Hill, Plymouth. A record exists of her arrival at Falmouth from Truro on December 12 1930, and shows that Westcott ships were arriving or departing from Falmouth on the same tide. A commonplace entry, but a cameo of an age now past.

The *JNR* spent her working life in the coastal waters of the West Country, and ceased trading in the early 1950s. For a while she was then used as a mobile café based on Falmouth. Between 1957 and 1960 she was converted to a private yacht. During World War II she was employed at Plymouth as a barrage balloon vessel. In 1947, when HMS *Warspite* was wrecked off St Michael's Mount while on tow to the breakers, the *JNR* spent 12 months ferrying men and materials to and from the wreck.

In 1970 her present owner, Mr Eric Paull, saw her, quite by chance, at Shoreham, Sussex, and purchased her. Much time and money was spent in the following years converting her, but now Eric and his Alsatian 'Smokey' have the *JNR* as their home. She has a saloon 16ft × 10ft, two double cabins, two single berths in the forecastle, a bathroom, galley with calor gas cooker and Aga cooker which provides constant hot running water, and three systems of heating and lighting – calor gas, mains electricity, and a 12 volt battery. But the *JNR* is no mere houseboat. She frequently puts to sea and has taken her owner to many English Channel ports from Rochester to Falmouth. No longer, however, does she spread her sails. Today she is powered by a 2-ton 66hp diesel engine, but carries a steadying sail on the foremast. Her mizzen carries a radar aerial.

'*JNR* is built like a battleship', says Eric Paull. Carrying the heavy diesel engine has caused no problems, and although she has twice been rammed in harbour by merchant ships, only very minor damage has been sustained.

In 1972 the *JNR* was visited by Captain RCC Greenless of the Maritime Trust, who are anxious that this old vessel should not pass into foreign hands, and would like a first opportunity to purchase, if her owner ever considers sell-

J.N.R. *last surviving Plymouth smack at Weir Quay.* Martin Langley.

ing. She is now based at Weir Quay on the Tamar, and effectively gaurded by the vociferous 'Smokey'.

Official number: 102421. Tonnage: 41 gross, 34 net. Length: 58·3ft × beam 18·2ft × depth 6·6ft.

Ketch *Garlandstone*
(Afloat and being restored)

This 76-ton ketch can be seen in the course of a five-year restoration at Morwellham Quay, on the east bank of Tamar. Launched in 1909 she was built on speculation at the former Goss Shipyard, Calstock. There she took the fancy of Captain JD Russan, a Welsh owner/skipper, who bought her, registered her at Milford Haven, and put her to work in the coastal and continental trade. In 1912 she was fitted with a 40ihp oil engine but her sail area was not reduced. Undoubtedly her most heroic voyage was in 1940 when her crew, expecting destruction by mine or U-boat, refused to sail her from a south Ireland port to Lydney. Her then captain, named Murdoch, was undaunted. Though *in his seventies*, he sailed her single-handed on the 48-hour voyage, defying the minefields. It was a remarkable feat. He then sold her to a refugee Polish shipmaster who continued to work her in the Bristol Channel and Irish Sea trade. In 1956 she was sold to an American at Braunton for a yacht, but this conversion never took place and the *Garlandstone* lay semi-derelict until acquired by the National Museum of Wales. She was then towed to Porthmadoc where restoration began. Because of her association with the Port of Plymouth it was agreed that she should be based in the Tamar. She will be regularly on view at Morwellham Quay, but will make summer cruises to Wales, under sail.

Official number: 128746. Tonnage 76 gross, 54 net, 100 dead-weight. Length: 76·0ft × beam 20·2ft × depth 9·0ft.

Garlandstone *under tow approaching Morwhellam Quay on the Tamar where she is being restored.* Morwhellam Quay.

River Lynher

No boats for hire are available in the vicinity. By car, from Plymouth cross the Tamar Bridge and leave the A 38 at Landrake, for the *Millom Castle*, *Lynher* and *Maggie Annie*. For the *Lord John Roberts* take the St Stephens and Forder road after crossing Tamar Bridge. For the *Harry*

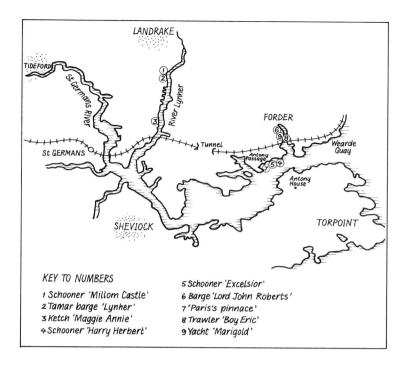

KEY TO NUMBERS

1 Schooner 'Millom Castle'	5 Schooner 'Excelsior'
2 Tamar barge 'Lynher'	6 Barge 'Lord John Roberts'
3 Ketch 'Maggie Annie'	7 'Paris's pinnace'
4 Schooner 'Harry Herbert'	8 Trawler 'Boy Eric'
	9 Yacht 'Marigold'

Herbert, *Excelsior* and *Paris*'s pinnace take the road from Saltash to Wearde Quay and walk along the foreshore during the latter half of the falling tide.

River Lynher (West Bank)

Tops'l Schooner *Millom Castle* & Tamar Barge *Lynher*

Millom Castle The last resting-place of this fine old schooner is reached by leaving the A 38 Plymouth-Liskeard road at Landrake village and taking the left hand fork after passing the church, to Poldrissick Farm. Here permission must be obtained to take the private footpath to Poldrissick Quarry, where the ship lies with her stern against the bank.

Millom Castle was built as a tops'l schooner at Ulverton in 1870 for William Postlethwaite of Millom, Cumberland; and was one of the Postlethwaite fleet of 23 trading schooners. Very sturdily built, she had 2½in pine strakes topsides and elm below the bilges. Her frames, floors and futtocks were of oak, and her 10in deck beams of hackmatack. She survived storm damage in March 1905, when her crew of three and a dog were taken off by the Tenby lifeboat *William and Mary Dever*. After 42 years service

The end of a hard-worked old ship: Millom Castle *at Poldrissick Quarry.* Martin Langley.

she was sold in 1912 to WK Slade of Appledore, who installed an auxiliary engine seven years later.

Her career in the Slade fleet is quite fully documented by Captain WJ Slade in his book *Out of Appledore* (Conway Maritime Press 1972). Read his account of how the *Millom Castle*, while heavily laden, weathered a 100mph gale in March 1922 in the Irish Sea, and you will look on her now ageing timbers with deep respect. In 1921 the Slades had converted her from tops'l schooner to ketch rig; and some years later altered her again to a three-masted fore-and-aft schooner. *Millom Castle* was always, both light and loaded, very handy under sail. She was normally handled by a crew of three, and in 1913 none of her crew, master included, was over 21 years of age!

In 1932 she was towed into Plymouth by the steam trawler *Atlantic* after an October gale left her dismasted and water-logged. She was now over 60 years old, and the Slades surrendered her that year. After survey she was registered as fit for harbour work only, and eventually made her last voyage up the River Lynher to her present resting-place. Here she has since been joined by the Tamar barge *Lynher*. Basil Greenhill, former director of the National Maritime Museum, has written of *Millom Castle*'s demise: 'She is reverting to nature very gracefully in her present quiet location, a very happy end to a hard-worked old vessel'.

Official number: 65043. Tonnage: 93 gross, 60 net.
Length: 81·2ft × beam 20·6ft × moulded depth 9·5ft.
Aux engine 40hp.

Lynher in the Lynher: the river provides a death-bed for its namesake. Martin Langley.

Lynher The Tamar barge *Lynher* has also found her graveyard in this now overgrown quarry she served so long as a stone carrier. Nature has so overtaken this one-time hive of industry, that a clear view of this old sailing barge can only be obtained by thrusting oneself through the riverbank bushes, or scrambling aboard the *Millom Castle* beside whose bow she lies, sunk almost to her bulwarks in the mud.

Lynher was built in 1891 by James Goss at Calstock, a typical single-masted Tamar barge, smack-rigged, with gaff and a large boom. Her duties were to be humble, for her 60 years of active life were mostly spent in the carriage of stone, timber, and Plymouth Dock dung. At one time, however, she was owned by Mr Brand of Tideford Post Office and Stores, and he employed her in bringing supplies up-river from his shop in Devonport.

For years after this the *Lynher* was engaged in the transport of stone from Poldrissick quarries, whose owners Steed Brothers had an interest in a number of similar Tamar barges, among them *Blue Elvan*, *Elizabeth Jane* and *Triumph*, all contemporary with *Lynher* in the stone traffic. Her last owner/skipper was Captain Sam Daymond of Saltash, who re-registered her in 1924 when she was fitted with an engine. His request to rename her *Britannia* was refused, presumably because Plymouth already had a trawler registered in that name. In December 1930 she made a sea voyage from Plymouth to Fowey. It is believed she was last at work in 1952, though possibly reduced by this time to a dumb lighter.

In 1972 there seemed a possibility of her restoration. It was said that the Navy, willing to assist in the project, had made a preliminary inspection. If so, the report was presumably unfavourable, as the idea was dropped in favour of other projects. Other people became interested and went to look at her. Once floated, it was pointed out, she was small enough to tow up to Tideford on a spring tide. When the National Trust initiated the restoration of the more pretentious barge *Shamrock*, interest in funding work on the *Lynher* understandably evaporated. The *Lynher* however is a more typical workaday Tamar barge, and if floated successfully, could probably be restored at proportionally less cost than eventually proved necessary for *Shamrock*. She would make a valuable addition to the restored Morwellham docks. But her hold is entirely filled with mud and she lies deep with little 'freeboard', so that expense would be involved before a verdict on her condition could be given.

Official number: 146000. Tonnage: 29 gross, 20 net, 60 dead weight. Length: 51·2ft × beam 17·5ft × moulded depth 5·4ft. Aux engine 26hp.

Ketch *Maggie Annie* SX 380584

Unless you own your own boat, and are willing to navigate (from Plymouth) across the Tamar estuary and up the River Lynher – about 7 miles – the *Maggie Annie* must be visited on a weekday during working hours. This is because the old ship lies at Treluggan Quarry, to which there is no land access from noon on Saturdays to 8 am Mondays. Permission to enter the quarry must be obtained from the quarry owner or foreman: but although one can look down on the hulk from 20 yards distance, it is only possible to board her by scrambling down a very rough bank.

Maggie Annie, a wooden ketch, was built in FJ Carver's yard at Bridgwater, Somerset, in 1881. Prior to the Great War she was engaged in general trade and owned by William Drake of Braunton. During the war she was sold to Frederick G Corney, of Wrafton; and in the 'twenties was owned by Foster Brothers of Plymouth, with Graham Foster as skipper and deep-sea sailor Jack Birch of Oreston as mate. Her principal employment then was in the stone

The survivor. Undaunted by bomb, fire and dynamite: the Maggie Annie *in retirement at Treluggan.* Martin Langley.

trade, running from quarries on the Tamar, Lynher, or Plym rivers to Fareham and Portsmouth.

Maggie Annie continued sailing until World War II, when she was laid up in Treluggan quarry. In 1941 she suffered blast damage from a German bomb which detonated on the river surface. Her engine was taken out and her masts and spars removed. One of her spars is still used in the quarry as a buffer-stop for lorries. The *Maggie*'s drive-shaft and propellor were left in her and are still intact.

In the 'drought summer' of 1976 the gorse on the adjacent bank caught alight and set fire to the ship, consuming the remains of the main deck. The quarry owner later tried demolishing her for firewood, placing 10 small sticks of dynamite in the hull. This assault however had a negligible effect on the sturdy *Maggie Annie* and today the proprietor rather enjoys telling this story against himself! The old ketch may look in a sorry state today but she was very soundly built, her timbers are dowelled, hardly any nails being used.

Official number: 78706. Tonnage: 79 gross 69 net, 100 dead weight. Length: 76·5ft × beam 20·2ft × depth 9·0ft.

River Lynher (North Bank)

Sailing Barge *Lord John Roberts*   SX 413578

The grandeur of the name belies the humble nature of the craft which is slowly mouldering in Forder Creek: for she was a sailing barge engaged on mundane duties, and so far as is known, never ventured beyond the port limits of Plymouth. She was single-masted and smack or lugger rigged, and her chainplates are still in position. The date of her building is uncertain but Jack Crosley, boat proprietor, river pilot and retired ferryman, believes it was about 1900–02. He is certainly the most reliable authority today on nautical matters concerning the Lynher, and knows this barge well enough. He says 'I don't remember her ever being in trade. She spent much of her life working out of HM Dockyard'.

The Mercantile Navy List chronicles a lugger-rigged vessel named *Lord Roberts* (ON 121645) in 1928, built at Sandhaven in 1900 of about the right size (33 tons net) but registered and owned at Lerwick. Could this be the vessel that found her way to Devonport Dockyard by the 1930s?

During the 1950s she was sold, dismasted, to the Sea Scouts, and brought into Forder Creek to serve as headquarters and training vessel. She arrived with large iron deck bollards, which were removed and dumped by the shore nearer the head of the creek, where they can still be seen. In the event, the Sea Scouts made little use of her, and have long since disbanded. The *Lord John Roberts* was left to her fate, and to the mercy of timber-hunters and vandals. Her hulk is sometimes erroneously identified as the *Saltash* or *Village Belle*, Tamar barges of approximately the same size. Her bow and for'ard planking have gone, and at most stages of the tide it is easy to step into the hold. Her deck-planking has been taken up, and all that is left at deck level are the steel combings of her main hatch.

But in spite of the wreck's shortcomings as a showpiece, and lack of any thrilling history, most who come here will not regret it. For this is quite a beautiful spot, remote from 'the madding crowds', its peace disturbed only by the mainline trains crossing the lofty Forder Viaduct, and the chug of the occasional passing motor-boat.

Yacht *Marigold*   SX 413577

The yacht Marigold *ashore at Forder. She came here for restoration but it becomes increasingly unlikely that she will return to her element.* Edwina Small.

Standing forlornly ashore in a wooden cradle, between the floating *Boy Eric* and the tidal *Lord John Roberts*, the cutter *Marigold* has been at Forder Creek since October 1982. Built by Nicholson's at Gosport in 1882 as a yacht with gaff rig, her best years belong to the golden days of yachting

when, though clubs and events and yachts were proliferating, it was still the sport of rich men.

In 1928 the long tradition of gaff-rigged yachts was challenged by the new *Astra* with a tall mast supporting a triangular mainsail. *Marigold* was altered to this 'Bermudan' rig the following year. In 1930 she was sailed by David Niven, later to become famous as the star of Wuthering Heights, The Guns of Navarone, and many other films.

Her present owner, Gregory Powlesland, found *Marigold* lying semi-derelict in a creek of the Isle of Wight, and arranged for her transport by road to Torpoint. He estimated the cost of her restoration at £50,000 and expected to spread the work over four years. *Marigold* was the subject of a Television South West news item on October 25 1982, when it was stated that it was hoped to move the vessel into a boat shed the following month. Now it seems that plans have miscarried, for though the deck is partly protected by sheets of galvanised iron, no work is proceeding and the hull is deteriorating .

Tonnage: 30 gross. Length: 39ft

Trawler *Boy Eric*　　　　　SX 414576

This former Lowestoft trawler is today in a sorry state, secured to the railway viaduct in Forder Creek; and though said to be under repairs, looks unlikely to put to sea again.

She was built at Rye in 1921 by G & T Smith Ltd, builders of *Master Hand*, so her pedigree is immaculate. By this time steam trawlers were predominant, and the *Boy Eric* had a short life in fishing. The fates brought her west, and after a spell in the Brixham trawl fleet, she became a floating home for Brian Kent, later yard manager of Quayside Services, Stonehouse Pool, Plymouth. When this firm went into liquidation, *Boy Eric* was moored first in the Hamoaze, and later in the Cattewater, where she was sold, without benefit of survey, to Roger Lovejoy – who claims to be Jesus – for £11,500. With his Israeli wife and little daughter African Moon on board, her new owner brought her back to the Hamoaze in August 1984, but came into collision with the Cremyll Beacon, causing considerable damage to her starb'd bow. For some months she was secured to a Cory's buoy off Gravesend Beach, where her owner's claim to divinity suffered when it was observed that he needed a dinghy to get ashore. There was a flurry of excitement in October, when with the birth of a second child imminent, a police launch arrived alongside the *Boy Eric* bringing two nurses, and Mrs Lovejoy was embarked for transfer to the Torpoint Ferry, which was actually halted in midstream and awaited at Devonport slip by an

Boy Eric, *secured to the Forder Railway viaduct, hides the damage from her encounter with Cremyll Beacon.* Edwina Small.

ambulance. The babe, however, was born on the police launch and mother and child brought back to the *Boy Eric*.

Requests to beach the unseaworthy trawler at Torpoint being unavailing, recourse was made to Forder Creek where she has lain since.

ON 145779 Registered Lowestoft. Tonnage 24 net.

Steam Pinnace   SX 420574

In the small bay a few hundred yards upstream from Wearde Quay is the much-vandalised hull of a small steel vessel, difficult of access because of the mud. She looks unprepossing but is worth more than a passing glance, for she was a naval pinnace and is a mute reminder of the fall of France in 1940.

In June that year part of the French fleet arrived at Plymouth after avoiding the vigilance of the Germans. The battleship *Paris*, the giant submarine *Surcouf*, and attendant cruisers and destroyers rounded Drake's Island and came to berths in the Dockyard. Thousands of men packed the decks of the *Paris* and her masts and rigging supported hundreds more. JC Trewin (*Portrait of Plymouth*, Robert Hale 1973) records: 'Plymouth crowds looked on in silence: the French ships seemed dirty, almost slovenly, and many were patched with rust'. Within a fortnight, with suspicion growing that the ships might return to now-occupied France, British naval boarding-parties seized the ships, and there were fatal casualties on board the *Paris*. Some weeks after this, Dockyard staff lowered the *Paris*'s steam pinnace into the water, and brought her under her own power to this unlikely spot in the River Lynher, where they anchored and left her.

Jack Crosley, Antony-Forder ferryman and river pilot, paid her a visit and liked what he saw. He approached the Dockyard authorities with an offer to purchase, but was told the craft was not for sale. Much later, he received a visit from a police-sergeant, enquiring who owned the pinnace. 'The Dockyard' replied Jack, 'but why?' It appeared the sergeant had just arrested two youths for taking 60lbs of copper tubing and wire from the pinnace, which they had wrenched from her engine. Later the sergeant encountered Jack again. 'The Dockyard denied ownership and didn't want to know' he told him, 'so I shall let the lads go'.

With such official indifference to the vessel's fate, it is not surprising that she was soon ransacked for everything of value, and the *Paris* eventually returned to France minus her pinnace. The ravages of weather, tides, neglect and vandalism have since reduced a trim and seaworthy craft to a rusting, broken hulk.

Frenchman's Creek. Paris's pinnace in the quiet backwater where she was left to decay. Edwina Small.

Schooners *Harry Herbert* & *Excelsior*

SX 423576

The remains of these 19th century schooners lie side by side on the north shore, just upstream of Wearde Quay. It is necessary to go during the lower half of the tide, as the beach is covered at high water.

Harry Herbert This the more easterly of the two. Built at Rhyl in 1860, she was a sturdy, beamy schooner, registered at Liverpool. Little is known of her early history but by the turn of the century she had come into the owner-ship of Dennis J Murray of Court-macsherry, Co Cork. In the early 1920s she was sold to the Forward Lighterage Company Ltd of London, and traded in and from the Bristol Channel.

Harry Herbert, *the last resting place of this Liverpool-registered schooner.*

Her seagoing days were over when during World War II she was bought by Joe Haskell, shipping agent and coal factor of Plymouth, and moored in the Cattewater harbour as a coal hulk. The arrangements were primitive. Hand-winches and the ship's own gear were used to wind the coal from the hold in baskets, and it was then manhandled over gangplanks. In the 1950s she was towed to her last resting-lace in the Lynher, where she has since been vandalised for her timber. The wreck can be boarded at low water, and it can be seen that her kelson has two mast steps for'ard, indicating that the position of her foremast was altered at some time.

Official number: 28186. Tonnage: 128 gross 99 net.
Length: 83·9ft × beam 23·7ft × depth 11·6ft.

Excelsior A smaller schooner, she was built in 1875 in the Channel Islands. By 1902 she was working out of the Bristol Channel, owned by Richard G Foster, and managed by Alexander Johns of Gloucester Docks. By 1919 she had changed hands and was trading for David Williams of Gloucester. Her sale to the Forward Lighterage Company of London in the 'twenties brought her under the same flag as the *Harry Herbert*. Thereafter their fates were interwoven. She also was sold, at the same time, to Haskell of Plymouth for a coal hulk, and was regularly towed from her moorings, by Reynold's tugs, to bunker steamers at anchor in the Sound. Some years ago her hulk was set on fire, which hastened her disintegration.

Official number: 71851. Tonnage: 77 net. Port of Registry: London.

Other Ship remains in the Lynher

Immediately south of the *Harry Herbert* lie two narrow, steel barges, about 95ft in length. They were RN towed-target floats, which during World War II were used as boom-defence craft. Much of their hull-plating has been cut away.

Near the *Paris*'s pinnace are the keel and bilge timbers of what was probably a sailing barge, but is unlikely now to be identified.

At Antony Passage is the tidal hulk of a former RN picket boat, bought by a local resident for private use and now abandoned.

In Forder Creek, south of the railway viaduct, are the half-buried remains of a US landing craft of World War II.

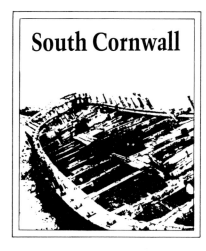

Looe River

Boy David

SX 247538

The fishing vessel *Boy David* lies on her port side under the trees of the north bank of West Looe River. None of her details are known, for she was not registered in the Mercantile Navy List. But it is known that she was locally built by a shipwright named Peter Ferris who in the 'twenties saw her at Porthleven, bought her and brought her back to Looe.

It was customary in sail days at Looe to lay up old craft in this stretch of river bank. At one time there were more than a dozen. A few years ago a lady wrote to a Looe Har-

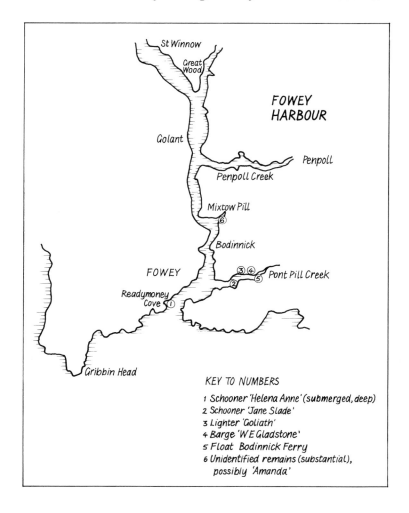

KEY TO NUMBERS

1 Schooner 'Helena Anne' (submerged, deep)
2 Schooner 'Jane Slade'
3 Lighter 'Goliath'
4 Barge 'W E Gladstone'
5 Float Bodinnick Ferry
6 Unidentified remains (substantial), possibly 'Amanda'

bour employee asking him to cut her a piece of wood from the *Boy David*: it transpired that her father had had the boat built by Peter Ferris. The request was complied with.

River Fowey

The ship-remains at Fowey have to be approached by water. So you must hire a boat (from Town Quay) or unload your car-borne dinghy. All small craft are required by harbour regulations to keep clear of the main channel and swinging ground.

Schooner *Jane Slade*

Originally rigged as a two-masted schooner, the *Jane Slade* was launched sideways at Fowey in May 1870, built by Christopher Slade and named after his wife. After his death that same year his widow took over the firm and completed the ship. Their son Thomas Slade became master. In 1905 the ship was re-rigged as a three-masted schooner, and later is reported to have made the fastest-ever voyage under sail from the Azores to Bristol. The *Jane Slade* was de-registered when 58 years old, in 1928, and laid up in Pont Pill. By the late 'thirties her decay was advanced, but her figurehead was removed and used to decorate the gable-end of 'Ferryways', Sir Gerald du Maurier's house at Bodinnick. Daphne Du Maurier wrote a novel centred around the ship – *The Loving Spirit*. The hulk was still visible at low water a few years ago, but whether showing or not today, her keel and floors must still be lying under the mud.

Official number: 63961. Tonnage: 149 gross, 115 net.
Length: 97·7ft × beam 22·9ft × depth 12·3ft.

Schooner *Helena Anna*

An old deep-sea trader that later transferred to coasting, the *Helena Anna* was built at Pekela, Holland in 1870 by Axel Drenth. A wooden three-masted schooner, partly copper-fastened, partly iron bolts, she was salted in 1897. In 1893 she became one of six vessels owned and managed by William Varcoe Kellow of Fowey, where she was thereafter registered. The others in Kellow's fleet were *Hebe*, *Maria*, *Sarah Lightfoot*, *Traveller* and *Tullockgorum*. Her

Helena Anna *in Pont Pill prior to World War II.* Cdr H Oliver Hill.

skipper prior to – and possibly during – the Great War was WH Brokenshire. In 1935 she was deemed time-expired, and laid up in Pont Pill, where she remained till 1940, masts and spars still standing. She was then commandeered by the Admiralty, and sunk as a blockship in Readymoney Cove at the Harbour entrance. The Harbourmaster tells us 'Divers say there are some remains but none visible at any state of the tide'.

Official number: 85257. Tonnage: 179 gross, 134 net.
Length: 106·2ft × beam 25·2ft × depth 11·7ft.

Ketch *Amanda*

The ketch Amanda *whose remains can be seen in Mixtow Pill, photographed in her heyday at Porthleven in the 1920s.* RHC Gillis, MPS.

The remains of the *Amanda* are in Mixtow Pill. She was built in 1867 by Willmott at Padstow, which remained her port of registry. As launched she was a two-masted schooner with a square stern, 'out-of-doors' rudder and tiller steering. In 1909 she was owned and skippered by

Henry House of Newquay. During the Great War she was acquired by the Stephens' fleet at Par. They sold her about 1920 to new owners who converted her to ketch rig *c* 1929. She was eventually abandoned at Fowey in the late 'thirties.

Official number: 58243. Tonnage: 97 gross, 87 net.
Length: 82·7ft × beam 21·3ft × depth 10.1ft.

Float *Bodinnick Ferry*

Built 1918 by Slades of Fowey for Landlord Green of the Passage House (now Old Ferry) Inn, Bodinnick, who held the ferry rights at the time. Then known as the 'cow boat', it was an animal/waggon float, designed to be propelled with sweeps by a crew of two. The wreck lies on the south side of Pont Pill and is still in recognisable condition.

Lighter *Goliath*

Her remains still to be seen in Pont Pill, the *Goliath* was a coal tender owned by A Smith, a Fowey coal merchant. Being engineless, she was towed to and from bunkering ships by tug.

Barge *WE Gladstone*

Ketch-rigged, the *Gladstone* was built at St Ives in 1885, during that Liberal leader's second premiership. She was registered at Fowey and owned by Josiah Hunkin of Polruan, who employed her chiefly in bringing stone to Pont and Lerryn. Eventually abandoned in Pont Pill and still identifiable.

Official number: 131985. Tonnage: 23 net.

River Fal

All the remains numbered on the map are accessible by land though some, such as *WJC* are not visible at high water. *Heron* and *La Brunette* are in a boatyard so permission is necessary to view.

The waters of the Fal do not come under the administration of a single authority, the estuary being controlled by the Falmouth Harbour Commissioners, with a harbour-

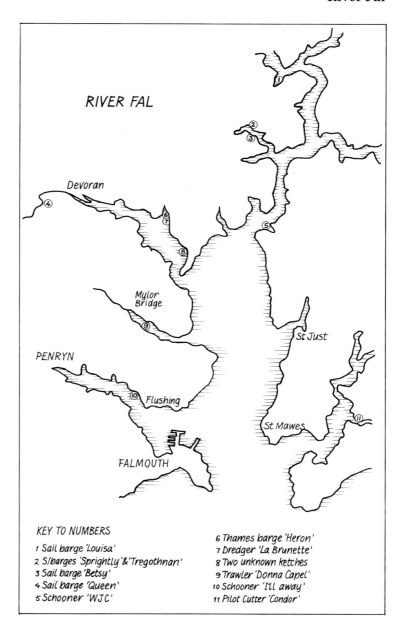

RIVER FAL

Devoran

Mylor
Bridge

St Just

PENRYN

Flushing

St Mawes

FALMOUTH

KEY TO NUMBERS

1 Sail barge 'Louisa'
2 S/barges 'Sprightly' & 'Tregothnan'
3 Sail barge 'Betsy'
4 Sail barge 'Queen'
5 Schooner 'WJC'

6 Thames barge 'Heron'
7 Dredger 'La Brunette'
8 Two unknown ketches
9 Trawler 'Donna Capel'
10 Schooner 'I'll away'
11 Pilot Cutter 'Condor'

master at Falmouth: and the upper reaches and Penryn river by the Carrick District Council, with harbourmasters at Truro and Penryn. In recent years both authorities have been zealous in shore clearance, so that today, with few exceptions, there are only keels and little more to be found, of dying ships.

Lamb Creek

Barge *Louisa*   SW 840420

Although *Louisa* was a smack-rigged trading barge, she was described as a 'lighter' by the men of Combe Creek nearby, who reserved the name 'barge' for their own Cowlands Shipyard craft. *Louisa*'s sternpost and fore-pillar are still standing and enough of her lower timbers and forefoot to suggest that she was once quite a handsome vessel of her kind. She is reached from the Calerick – Old Kea road by turning into a drive with a white gate marked Lamb's Creek House, and, leaving one's car at the gateposts of the second field, walking diagonally across the field to the head of the creek, where *Louisa*'s remains lie under overhanging trees.

Combe Creek

Barges *Sprightly* & *Tregothnan* (SW 832410) & *Betsy* (SW 832407)

These were all River Fal sailing barges, all built by Gunn Brothers at Cowlands shipyard. Their freight capacity was 25–30 tons and they principally carried coal, grain, or limestome ballast for sailing ships. They were smack-rigged, with a single mast, foresail and mainsail, the former secured to a short bumpkin. When removing ships' ballast, the barges dumped it on the banks of the Tresillian and Ruan rivers, and these dumps can still be seen. When rail transport monopolised their other cargoes, the Fal barges were dependent on providing the ballast service. The general adoption of water-ballast signalled the end of their usefulness. These barges whose remains now lie in Combe Creek were all laid up in thoroughly sound condition, and with masts and rigging standing, prior to World War I. Septuagenarian Gerald Dunn of Combe recalls scrambling aboard them as a boy, to play. They never moved again, and here gradually fell to pieces. Another, unidentified keel lies beside *Sprightly*.

Others of their type were the *Topsy* and *Kitty* of which no trace remains.

Devoran Creek

Barge *Queen* SW 778386

Built of wood by Charles Dyer of Malpas at Scoble & Davies yard, Sunny Corner in 1893, the *Queen* was a ketch-rigged Devoran sailing barge, and employed locally throughout her commercial life. Falmouth was her port of registry. Mr WJ Trebilcock of Truro remembers her working from there in later years with no topmast nor bowsprit and her rig cut down to mains'l and stays'l. This was between 1923 and 1927, for after 30 years under sail alone, the *Queen* was fitted with a 2hp auxiliary engine in 1923. Her work in trade ended *c* 1927, when she was acquired by Arthur S Williams of Mawes.

Arthur Williams, a retired solicitor, came to St Mawes from the East Coast in a small yacht, the *Ben-y-Cloe*. He bought the *Queen* at Malpas from the old yard where she had been built, and moved her to St Mawes, where a long cabin was built on her maindeck by Frank Peters of Polrarth, *c* 1927–8. Mr Peters remembers carrying out this work, and says that 'about 1929 Mr Williams sailed the *Queen* around the Spanish coast and won a prize awarded by the Cruising Contact Association for long-distance sailing'. After Williams' death at Falmouth, the *Queen* was bought by another yachtsman named Thomson. She changed hands for the last time when sold to a local man who moored her near the Norway Inn, Perranarworthal, as a houseboat. About 1964–5 she broke her back on a mudbank and was abandoned where she now lies.

Official number: 146332. Tonnage: 24·9 gross, 8·52 net. Length: 46·6ft × beam 13·4ft × depth 5·2ft. Draught: 3·7ft. Engine: Bergius paraffin 2-cylinder.

Tolcarne Creek

Schooner *WJC* SW 839384

Nearly a mile south of King Harry Ferry, the remains of the wooden coastal trader *WJC* lie in Tolcarne Creek. To reach the spot, leave the B 3289 at the turn to Garwarthen, whence a long lane, constructed by American forces in World War II, leads down to Turnaware Point. The *WJC* was built as a schooner by Dyer of Truro in 1880. Nothing is known of her early years, but she was salted (except for the beams) in accordance with Regulation 37 for wood ships, and was fastened with iron bolts. Prior to the Great War she was owned by J James of Truro (where she was registered) with NB Buller as manager. During the war she plied regularly across the Channel to France with coal cargoes. Her rig was later cut down to ketch, probably during the 'twenties. Latterly she was owned by a Capt Cook and his brother, and it is said that when disagreements decided them on dissolving partnership, the *WJC* was put ashore here, after a return trip to France, all standing, and left to rot. The brothers could not agree about her disposal, and each was too proud to remove any of her fittings. This was about 1936 and the ship remained abandoned till she began to fall apart. Much of her timber was then dismantled and taken away for other uses. Her starb'd navigation lamp has been salvaged and preserved in private ownership. Even today, determined shovelling might bring some artefacts to light. The *WJC*'s remains lie in about two feet of liquid mud, her dolly winch still standing out at low water, while her pump – windlass and chains lie sprawled in the ooze.

Official number: 78969. Tonnage: 86 gross, 78 net.
Length: 79·2ft × beam 20·8ft × depth 9·5ft.

Penpol Creek

Sprits'l barge *Heron*   SW 813387

In this small inlet on the northside of Restronguet Creek can be found one of a small number of Thames sprits'l barges which have sought retirement in the West Country. This is the *Heron* which for some years has been forming part of the breakwater for the Penpol boatyard.

In these pages we have already encountered the *Bertie* at Plymouth, and have yet to consider the *Maggie* at Hayle and *Shamrock* at Appledore, but the Society of Sprits'l Barge Research believe that two others have ended their days in the SW – the *Julia* at Highbridge, and the *Violet Sybil* in the Kingsbridge Estuary. (Any information from readers about either of these veterans' fate will be welcomed by the authors).

Registered at London, the *Heron* was built at Greenhithe in 1899 for J Bevon of Northfleet. Bevon was a cement manufacturer, and his cement works and fleet eventually became part of APCM – the Associated Portland Cement Manufacturers. After nearly 28 years in the cement trade. *Heron* was sold to an owner/skipper named Edward Butcher in 1927.

Heron had been one of the Portland Company's largest and best barges, and she fetched a price of £745 according to Frank Wilmott in his book *Cement, Mud, and Muddies*. Trading in general cargoes in the Thames and Medway, *Heron* worked 20 years for her new owner. Her last skipper had been mate of the barge *Enchantress* when she sank in a November gale in 1921. In 1947 the *Heron* was sold for conversion to a barge-yacht. She may then have acquired a deckhouse, but as built her cabin-space was all below deck. A distinguishing feature was her short helm-wheel shaft; but we have not yet had an opportunity to board the hulk and note whether this is still evident.

Official number: 110174. Tonnage: 64 net.

Dredger *La Brunette*   SW 813386

This unprepossessing dredger-sludgeboat was built in 1906 on the Gironde estuary in France as a humble dumb-barge. After World War II, life took on a new dimension for her, in spite of her 40 years. A Brittany shipyard lengthened her by 30 feet and installed two Baudoin DK3 diesel engines. She was then used as a sand and calcified seaweed dredger in Brittany, fitted with a crane which she carried till 1981.

In 1976 she was sold to the Roselyon Shipping Company, Ltd, Cornwall, for seaweed-dredging and sludge-carrying purposes. Disaster came on the night of the 24/25 April 1981 when she sprang a leak and sank in the Fal at King Harry Reach. Her crew were ashore, and their dismay was complete when they intended to board her in the morning and saw only her mast protruding apologetically above the water! She was refloated on May 12 and towed to Newham Quay, where she became tidal.

Mr David Cary, director of Cornish Calcified Seaweed Ltd, told us that *La Brunette* was sold by them in 1981 for a nominal sum to Alex Howat who was intending to convert her to a houseboat. Had these plans materialised, it would have been a remarkable third lease of life for a humble vessel over 75 years old. By the end of '81 *La Brunette* had been refloated and was towed downstream to Penpol boatyard. Here the attempt to make her a habitable houseboat understandably failed, and she has joined *Heron* as tidal breakwater.

Length: 94·15ft × beam 20·8ft × depth 9·32ft. Tonnage: 97·98 gross, 48·27 net.

Restronguet Creek

Two unknown ketches   SW 817377

On the north bank of the creek, opposite the Pandora Inn, are the keels of two old ketches, whose identity is now a mystery. They were beached here by a Tim Ferris, who broke them up for their copper fastenings.

Sailor's Creek

This creek in the Penryn river may be said to be haunted by the ghosts of old ships. A falling tide exposes keels, floors, and general wreckage, but nothing complete enough to be termed a hulk. The scattered remains include:

Schooner *Earl Cairns* (127 tons, 1883)
Cutter-rig barge *Silex* (25 tons, 1898)
Brigantine *Volant* (167 tons, 1867)
Clipper *Berean* (526 tons, 1869)
Barque *Gurli* (748 tons, 1879)
Lugger *Alice*
Fairmile W/W II MTB

The 167-ton brigantine Volant *drying her sails at anchor. Her bones now lie in Sailor's Creek near Flushing.*

Forty years later. Her frames collapsed, Earl Cairns *lies spreadeagled in Sailor's Creek.* Martin Langley.

The Earl Cairns *in 1938. She is shown here berthed at Cattedown, Plymouth.* Cdr H Oliver Hill.

Mylor Creek

Trawler *Donna Capel* SW 807357

Dismasted and stripped of gear, the hull of the trawler *Donna Capel*, still seaworthy when we last saw her, lies on the mud of the south bank of Mylor Creek, near the boatyard of ECLP Gaffers and Luggers. It was late on a July evening when we found her, and an overcast, darkening sky discouraged photography. Oyster fishing boats kept her company; some, astern of her, trim and buoyant on their moorings; others derelict on the strand close by. We assumed that *Donna Capel* was awaiting conversion to a yacht or houseboat, and we later wrote to the boatyard for confirmation, but received no reply.

Donna Capel was built at Ostend, Belgium, in 1943 during the gravest days of World War II. She fished in the continental waters for 18 years, and was sold to Brixham in 1961. There she was re-registered with the port mark BM 142 and remained for several years; but her subsequent story, and how she came to Mylor Creek, remain a mystery.

Length: 46·7ft × beam 13·8ft × depth 6·1ft.

Flushing Beach

Schooner *I'll Away* SW 807338

Only the keel, ribs and some planking remain of this old Fowey-registered schooner. On February 4 1915 she survived a storm in the Bristol Channel when she dragged her anchors two miles off a lee shore and had to summon the lifeboat with distress flares. The Swansea/Mumbles lifeboat *Charlie Medland* rescued the crew of three. Ralph Bird of Carnon Mine recalls her hull being bought by John Eddy, a local shipwright, for her scrap metal. He began breaking her up but was disappointed for copper rivets – she was iron-fastened throughout. Thereafter she was abandoned – and gradually fell apart.

Percuil Creek

Cutter *Condor* SW 861343

Condor, built in 1874 at Percuil, was one of 13 pilot cutters then operating from Falmouth. She was converted to a yacht after steam cutters replaced sail, and was laid up

Top left: The end is nigh. Remains of the Fal pilot cutter Condor *at Percuil Creek.* Edwina Small.

Compton Castle is now a restaurant at Lemon Quay, Truro. Here she is in her prime on the Dart.

here during World War II. Her remains, consisting of keel, lower ribs, forefoot, and sternpost with transom and locker, lie only yards from the Gerrans – Percuil road.

Official number : 72486. 32 registered tons.

SS *Compton Castle* SW 828448

The paddler *Compton Castle*, now a floating restaurant at Truro, was the sixth of eight steamers purpose-built for the Totnes service by the River Dart Steamboat Company. Launched by Cox's of Falmouth a few months before the Great War broke out in 1914, she gave 48 years service on the river – the longest serving of the company's fleet. When the passenger service was discontinued during World War II, the *Compton Castle* was commandeered as an ammunition carrier, but still on the Dart. In peacetime hundreds of romances must have begun and blossomed on her wide decks.

Flying a 'paying-off pennant', and crowded with passengers, the steamer made her last river trip in September 1962 and was then laid up. The BBC hired her briefly for an appearance in the TV series The Onedin Line. In 1964 she was acquired by joint owners, Messrs Duck and Burt, and taken to Kingsbridge Quay. They used her as a floating cafe in the summer seasons, and nourished hopes of

The Compton Castle *ashore prior to her conversion.*

reconditioning her. Eventually the South Hams Council questioned the soundness of her hull plating, and fears were expressed that she might sink at her berth. For more than two years rows dragged on between the ship's successive owners and the Council, who finally demanded the removal of the ship by April 1, 1978. In fact it was May 19 before she sailed, and in the meantime, she was acquired by Cornish publican Ernie Clayton, who arranged to have *Compton Castle* towed to Looe. Harbourmaster Captain Jim Blazeby supervised her departure and a small crowd assembled to see her move out into the stream at high water.

The old steamer confounded her critics by weathering the long tow past the Eddystone without untoward incident. With her funnel and wheel house dismantled and lashed on deck, she safely negotiated the low arches of the Town Bridge at Looe and was berthed at East Looe. Ernie Clayton planned to spend £70,000 on a two-year restoration to passenger-carrying standards and then return the ship to her original work on the River Dart with his son Michael Clayton as skipper. A year later the vessel was towed up the West Looe River and put ashore on the west bank. Here some of her badly corroded bottom plates were removed before work came to a stop.

In the spring of 1981 it was reported that David Worledge, a Truro businessman, had plans to purchase the ship and moor her at Truro as a licensed restaurant. This proved true, and the *Compton Castle* was refitted at Looe before her tow to Truro. Customer patronage proved disappointing and eventually the restaurant closed and for months the ship lay disused in her confined berth at Lemon Quay. Under new management the restaurant reopened in 1986. Despite the gastronomic delights the old ship may have to offer, she will disappoint the shiplover who visits her. Tophamper clutters her decks, her new funnel does not look genuine, her engines have been removed (to the Isle of Wight Maritime Museum) and her paddle blades have not been replaced.

Official number: 130189. Tonnage: 97 gross, 52 net. Length: 108·0ft × beam 17·6ft × depth 3·0ft. Engines: 2-cyl 24hp. Speed: *c* 9 knots.

Tug *St Denys* ex-*Northgate Scot*

(Afloat and restored)

This Scottish-built steam tug spent all the 52 years of her working life as a harbour tug at Falmouth. Purpose-built to the order of the Falmouth Towage Company in 1929, she was bought in 1981 by the Falmouth Maritime Museum to preserve her from scrap and put her on public display. Her original name of *Northgate Scot* had been changed to *St*

The Pensioner. With funnel weather-capped, St Denys *reposes near the arena of her working life.* Falmouth Maritime Museum.

Denys in 1959 when all Falmouth tugs were named after Cornish saints.

Manned by a crew of seven, the ship had only five captains during her long working life. Her mooring, when awaiting duty, was off Trefusis Head near Flushing. Sid Cutler, now retired in Falmouth, recalls his days as her fireman, from 1945–55. 'Those were very busy times', he says, 'Plenty of shipping. Average 14 jobs a day – moving off wharves and docking and maybe taking a ship up or down the Fal. We used to bunker 40 tons of coal about every three weeks. Bunkering was done by myself and second engineer, 20 tons port and starb'd. I can safely say I was the only fireman to stay on that boiler for 10 years – because the boiler was not man enough for the size of the engine.' He remembers an accident to another tug with which they were working: '*Northgate Scot* was bow tug, as always. We had the *British Sailor* (5576 tons, 1918) on the Eastern Wharf – just finished tank cleaning. The tug *Lynch* (211 tons, 1924) came up to make fast and push up to keep *British Sailor* against the wharf. *Lynch* drifted back on to the tanker whose engines were moving. Her propellors took the side out of the *Lynch* in her engine room'. Fortunately there was no loss of life. *Northgate Scot* stood by the sunken tug for several days, divers using her salvage pump in the refloating task. In the early hours of February 1 1947 the United States steamer *Henry Middleton*, homeward bound from Cherbourg, ran ashore at Trefusis Point. Sid Cutler recalls that night – a SE'ly gale, and drenching rain. *Northgate Scot* pulled the ship clear after the Falmouth lifeboat *Crawford & Constance Conybeare* had taken the towing hawser across.

A unique feature of the ship is that she has the only Caprotti-valve marine engine now in existence. Her towing hook is slightly for'ard of midships, enabling her to turn easily, and reducing the danger of being pulled over or 'girded' – a mischance which overtook the Falmouth tug *St Levan* in 1960. She is equipped with a 200-yard jet fire monitor and a salvage pump with suction/discharge pipes for fire-fighting or pumping out a casualty. During World War II the tug was moored at Prince of Wales Pier, and pumped water to the Recreation Ground, 200 feet above sea level and half a mile distant.

Let Sid Cutler have the last word on his old ship: 'She has done her work well'.

Tonnage: 280 gross, 1·05 net. Length: 97·0ft × beam 25ft. Engine: 790ihp, 115rpm.

Lugger *Barnabas* (Afloat and restored)

Barnabas is a two-masted lugger and a survivor of a once numerous fleet of Cornish mackerel drivers. ('Drivers' is the Cornish word for drifters). She is a double-ender, a type developed in West Cornwall after the coming of the railway in the mid-19th century when the opening up of new markets inland created a demand for fast yet roomy vessels. The luggers' mackerel season began in January when the boats lay to drift nets up to 100 miles offshore. Before July the fleet separated in the quest for summer herring, some to the Irish coast, others to the North Sea. Pilchard fishing largely occupied the autumn, and in winter most of the fleet fished from Plymouth for herring. The railway, which had provoked the boom in Cornish drifting also destroyed it, for it attracted to the west Cornish ports over 100 East Coast trawlers which overfished the area and undermined the industry.

Barnabus was built at St Ives in 1881. Length: 36ft.

Helford River

Sailing Barge *Sunbeam*   SW 753277

The most significant hulk in the Helford River lies on the south bank of Porth Navas Creek, reached by a somewhat circuitous minor road from Constantine to Porth Navas village and thence by an unmetalled road skirting the river bank.

Although the name *Swift* has been mentioned in connection with this wreck, there seems little doubt that we have here the remains of the sailing barge *Sunbeam* built at Looe, in 1913. The 1929 Mercantile Navy list records her owner at that time as Alan S Gulstone of Salcombe, but her port of registry was Plymouth.

For years she carried grain landed at Falmouth Docks to the various mills which once operated at Truro, Malpas and Gweek in the Helford River. Her load capacity was between 30 and 40 tons. In 1921 she was registered, apparently for the first time, when she was given an auxiliary engine of 7hp. The date of her abandonment is uncertain, but local residents seem to agree that it was just before World War II – probably in 1937 or '38.

Official number: 145991. Tonnage: 10 gross 7 net (prior to engine), 8 net (as auxiliary). Length: 33·8ft × beam 11·6ft × depth in hold 5.4ft.

Newlyn Harbour

Fishing vessel *Pioneer* (Afloat and at work)

Beyond doubt the little *Pioneer* is one of the most interesting veterans in the south-west. Built in 1899 by Paynter's of St Ives as a 35ft steamboat, she was owned in her early days by a Mr Hendy who later had her lengthened to 43 feet by bisecting the hull and adding 8ft length amidships. She was then used to run sea excursions from the extension pier at Penzance to Lamorna Cove. At the cove Mr Hendy erected a gantry and pontoon enabling *Pioneer* to embark or land passengers whatever the tide but this had to be removed at the end of the summer season.

Later the *Pioneer* was converted into a midget steam trawler and fishing has since remained her principal employment. In 1940 she went to Falmouth to muster for the Dunkirk evacuation, but was not accepted because the

The fishing steamer Pioneer *at Porthleven early this century. She still survives as a motor salvage vessel at Newlyn.* RHC Gillis.

quantity of coal she would have had to carry on deck would have negated her passenger capacity. Her steam engine, of which, unfortunately, no details survive, was replaced in 1946 by a 44hp Kelvin motor. In 1952 the Kelvin in turn made way for a 30hp Lister.

Pioneer came into the possession of her present owner, Cyril Gascoigne, in 1966. After fishing as a long-liner she was used as a diving boat for crawfish, and has since done some salvage work on wrecks. The loss of her funnel has of course detracted from her appearance, but she now has a wheelhouse aft, while her grey-painted hull carries the postmark PZ 277. Her 'home' is alongside North Pier in Newlyn Harbour.

Tonnage: 9½ gross. Length: 43ft × beam 9ft × depth 4·8ft.

Trawler *Excellent* ex-*Efficient*
(Article contributed by W Stevenson, her owner).

Efficient was built in 1931 by J & G Forbes of Sandhaven for the Ritchie brothers, at that time engine manufacturers: eager to get their new revolutionary diesel engine on the market, they would help finance some owners. This is how *Efficient* was born as a revolutionary drifter, economic and fast. At that time most drifters were either coal burning or smaller petrol paraffin converted from sail.

Efficient worked from Fraserburgh and Lowestoft herring catching. What happened I don't know, but in 1935 she was put up for sale. Father and Uncle bought her. I think the reason this sale came about was because at that time Uncle was an agent for Petters of Yeovil, now Westlands, who were the owners of *Efficient*'s 160hp Petter Atomic Diesel Engine.

She was brought to Newlyn by skipper William Love who worked her from Newlyn lining in summer and herring catching in winter from Newlyn and Lowestoft. At that time most boats of 80ft and over that were trawling were steam or sail but some of the sail boats were being converted to motor because Lowestoft had seen the Ostende fleet of motor trawlers and started building with success, so Father decided to try his luck.

Efficient started trawling in 1938 under the command of Lowestoft skipper J Carr who was an experienced trawler skipper. *Efficient* was successful but her engine gave trouble on lots of occasions. The engine manufacturers' engineer sailed with her for some full trips to get the engine right and to gain experience for future Petter engines.

Efficient had to stop for a short while because her bulwarks were too low and a local firm heightened them. This was the first of *Efficient*'s many face changes. *Efficient*

'Home is the sailor, home from the sea'. Stevenson's Excellent. *PZ 513, berthed at Newlyn's North Pier in 1986.* Edwina Small.

kept trawling until 1940–41 under the same skipper. In that time she answered a call to Dunkirk but was recalled being too far away. She was dive-bombed once, machine-gunned once or twice and caught up in action with German E-boats that were attacking a British convoy. In that action two trawlers were put out of action, one being sunk, the other being de-masted.

At that time a big proportion of the English and Scottish fishing fleets were being or had been taken over for war service, so I think Father decided she would be safer there. So for the next four years *Efficient* became the property of the War Department, Father being paid £36 per month.

In 1945 at Grimsby she was de-requisitioned. By now she had broken her crankshaft so that ended the association with Petters. She was re-built after service as all other trawlers were so she was fitted with a 160hp Blackstone Lister. Father preferred a 200hp but at that time engines were scarce. Father also changed her name to *Excellent* PZ 513 and in 1946 she started fishing again as fish were plentiful. Then she went lining again under skipper J Reynolds and had a successful year. After the season Father changed her back trawling again, so from 1947 she has, except for one summer, been trawling ever since.

The firm of W Stevenson owns 15 trawlers so lots of skippers started on *Excellent* and moved on to other bigger ships in our firm. Skipper Reynolds was superseded by skipper J Greengrass, T Lockwood and L Dew. In 1961 she was extensively modernised again, being stripped to deck level. She was then fitted with her third engine, a 280hp Mirlees Blackstone, going back to sea under skipper T Symons for two years. She was then skippered by her longest serving skipper E Hunter until 1970 when she was taken over by W Turrel. For a while she had a succession of trainee skippers for a year or two, then she was skippered by T Richards. *Excellent* was under the command of T Richards when she was inspected by the Queen as the oldest serving ship in the Newlyn fleet. Skipper Hunter was also presented as the oldest skipper. *Excellent* was to have another change of skipper again after T Richards' death on the Penlee Lifeboat with skipper Hunter until his retirement this year.

Excellent has had a varied career taking pictures of the *Flying Enterprise*, towing dragoons for Dunlop Rubber Company, helping to spread detergent after the *Torrey Canyon*, searching for a missing fighter for the Fleet Air Arm which she found on the sea bed by towing her trawl, going out in the Atlantic to search for the lone sailor in *Tinkerbell* and then taking his wife out to meet him.

Official number: 125368. Tonnage: 66·12 gross, 27·05 net. Length: 82ft (OA) 75ft × beam 18ft 4in × depth 10ft 6in. Engine: Mirlees Blackstone 280hp.

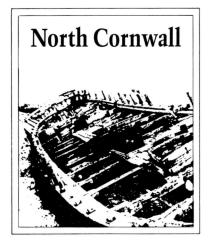

North Cornwall

River Hayle

It does not seem easy to hire a boat at Hayle which is scarcely a resort; but those carrying their own dinghy on car roof or trailer could use it to advantage in the bight of the estuary, if the tide is half flood or higher. The remains at the river mouth are most easily approached by land. Leave the car by Lelant Church and take the public footpath across the golf links and under the railway.

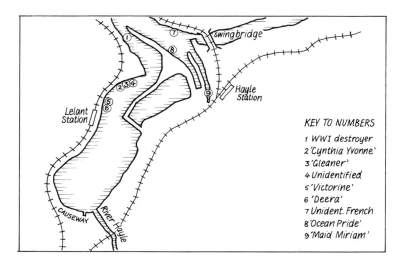

KEY TO NUMBERS

1 WWI destroyer
2 'Cynthia Yvonne'
3 'Gleaner'
4 Unidentified
5 'Victorine'
6 'Deera'
7 Unident. French
8 'Ocean Pride'
9 'Maid Miriam'

Small Lugger *Turtle*

Having parked at Lelant Church, and walked to the end of the footpath, turn right along the shore. The first remains you will encounter – if they have not been cleared by then! – are those of the *Turtle*, a small double-ended St Ives lugger, latterly used as a houseboat. She had been indiscreetly moored and was smashed up in a gale, winter 1977/8. *Turtle* was a renaming. There is no record of her original name.

Unknown Destroyer   SW 549379

Barely 200 yards beyond the *Turtle* will be seen the remains of a small warship embedded in the sand embankment. TW Ward, long-established shipbreakers of Gray's, Essex, used Lelant Quay for extensive shipbreaking of

The remains of a World War I Torpedo Boat Destroyer, possibly a veteran of Jutland.

redundant vessels after the Great War, from 1920 to 1932. The remains in the embankment are of an early Torpedo Boat Destroyer (with whaledeck for'ard) dismantled by Gray's. We have here not a complete hull, but a large section of the port side deeply embedded in the sand, and an area of superstructure plating, with scuttles still in position, retaining the bank. Other projections from the sand are less easily identified. These portions of the ship were built into the river bank in 1920 as a deterrent to erosion. It is impossible now to establish her identity but she may well be a veteran of Jutland.

Lugger *Cynthia Yvonne*   SW 548373

'Some achieve greatness, and some have greatness thrust upon them'. Shakespeare's words might just have been applicable to the lugger *Cynthia Yvonne*, whose forlorn-looking hull lies on the mud at Lelant. As recently as 1974 an attempt was made to thrust greatness on this little vessel, and her name figured for a few days in the national newspapers: but the greatness eluded her, for she was found not equal to the role in which she had been cast.

Built the year after the Great War by Peake's of Newlyn as a motor fishing lugger, her original name was *Rosebud*. In 1930 she briefly hit the headlines when she sailed from Newlyn to Westminster with a petition against the proposed demolition of fishermen's cottages in Newlyn. She

A deceptively seaworthy-looking Cynthia Evonne *drawn up ashore in 1986, but destined never to sail again.* Edwina Small.

was not requisitioned during World War II, and appears in the 1941 Olsen's Fisherman's Almanack as still fishing, with the portmark PZ 87. Her change of name followed a change of ownership after the war. She was soundly constructed and gave 60 years of service at Newlyn, latterly as a diving-boat, before being withdrawn and put up for sale. In 1972, lacking maintenance, she sank at her moorings in the harbour and remained tidal for two years. None would have guessed that she was about to be dragged from obscurity to limelight.

In 1974 she was bought by Mr Douglas Woolley of the Titanic & Seawise Salvage Company, a consortium formed to make a salvage attempt on the sunken White Star Liner. Mr Woolley had the *Cynthia Yvonne* refloated and cleaned up, and began reconditioning her for her first task, a geographic survey mission to the wreck. The *Titanic*, which sank on April 15, 1912, lies two miles deep in Lat 41 46′N, Lon. 5014′W off the Grand Banks of Newfoundland. The sea-going locals at Newlyn did not rate very highly the *Cynthia Yvonne*'s chances of crossing the Atlantic; indeed there were some who said she would be lucky to reach the Lizard. The lugger was fitted with two diesel engines, one taken from a lorry, and one from a bus: neither engine was reliable. After two years immersion the hull had suffered from worm and other marine parasites, and a spokesman for the Newlyn Fishermen's Association considered that it would cost over £5000 to make the vessel seaworthy. Mr Woolley's consortium had the technical backing of two Hungarian marine scientists, and had spent nearly £3000 on research and negotiations: but the project had to be abandoned when it was realised that the *Cynthia Yvonne* was economically beyond refitting for such a task. She was taken to Hayle in 1975 and abandoned, but her nameboard has been preserved in private ownership.

Built: 1919. Registered tonnage: 38.

An unidentified French tunny boat, possible the Crisco.

Mystery Vessel and Lugger *Gleaner*

Between *Cynthia Yvonne* and the low water line is the complete, black-painted hull of a counter-stern trawler which bears neither name nor portmark and whose identity is unknown, even to the Harbourmaster. She lies with a list to starb'd, her bulwarks and taffrail much damaged, almost atop the keel and ribs of the *Gleaner*, a St Ives lugger abandoned here in the 1930s.

Lugger *Deera*

Against the Lelant quay near the railway station, lies the *Deera*, ahead of the German launch *Victorine*. A single-masted trawler with smack rig *Deera* was built at St Ives in 1894, for a Bideford owner. For years she fished in Bideford Bay, apparently unrecorded in the Mercantile Navy List, until brought to Hayle by a diver who wanted her for salvage work. She was never put to work, and has since been slowly falling apart. Her fishing portmark was BD 13.

An end to her labours. The Deera *at Lelant Quay, Hayle.* Edwina Small.

Thames Barge *Mahelah* ex-*Maggie* SW 545364

Before her destruction by fire, this former sprits'l barge converted to houseboat well repaid a visit, and her owners have always been most gracious to occasional visitors who were informed and genuinely interested. Built at Sandwich, Kent, in 1898, the *Maggie* was one of about 12 sailing barges launched there by Felton's. Registered in London, she ran mostly between Rochester and the Isle of Wight with grain, but some voyages took her further afield. On passage from Teignmouth, Devon, to Wygmael, Belgium, in the June of 1910, she survived a collision with the schooner *Faith*. The owners of *Maggie* went to Court for damages, but they lost the day and also lost an appeal.

About 1925 she featured in a poster published by *Old Motor* magazine of which at least one copy is still in

Ravaged by fire. No future now for Mahelah, *a sorry sight at Hayle.* Martin Langley.

existence. The poster shows the Thames near St Paul's, with the *Maggie*, her masts lowered for negotiating the bridges, moored to a buoy. In 1929 her owner/skipper is recorded as Horace Shrubsall, of Tunnel Wharf, East Greenwich. During World War II she was at Southampton, in use as an operations conference centre by the US forces. About 1954 she was acquired by Rear Admiral GWG Simpson, CB, CBE, who was retiring from the Navy to live at St Erth. He brought *Maggie* to Hayle as a barge/yacht, still fully rigged, and with engine. When it was no longer economic to maintain her as a seagoing craft, he had her partly dismantled, the engine removed, and sold her for a houseboat to her present owners. She was renamed *Mahelah*. A large deckhouse then covered the after two thirds of her length, providing a comfortable lounge whose centre feature was the hatch of her mainhold. The seating for the binnacle could be clearly seen. Below decks the original compartments were retained and tastefully fitted out, the white-enamelled doors and panelling preserving the spartan shipboard atmosphere without loss of comfort and elegance.

At 4am on a winter's morning in early 1978 she was badly damaged at her berth when the waters of Hayle were lashed by a nor'westerly gale. Her port side was hammered against the quay, and the foredeckhouse smashed. In August that year we found her still under repair at her berth. Her rudder lay detached in the mud astern. In 1985 she was accidently set on fire when workmen were burning rubbish nearby, and the for'ard two thirds of the ship was gutted. She is a forlorn sight today, but her stern is just visible from the A 30 Hayle – St Erth road at the Causeway.

Official number 188293. Registered tonnage: 63.
Length: 82ft.

Drifter *Ocean Pride* (Afloat and working)

The trim and beautifully maintained *Ocean Pride* (PZ 134) though registered and owned in Penzance is currently working, from Hayle. She was built by NH Peake & Sons of Newlyn in 1922 for the Brownfield family, who sailed her as a mackerel/pilchard drifter. She was rigged as a dipping lugger, with an auxiliary engine – probably a small Kelvin – aft. About 1930 this was replaced by twin Kelvins of 66hp, which necessitated the engine room being moved for'ard where the hull form was fuller. The fore-mast was re-stepped 6ft for'ard at this time.

During World War II the *Ocean Pride* was commandeered by the War Department but we have been unable to discover to what specific use she was put. The Penzance Harbourmaster believes that she has had 'a colourful history' and we are hoping that more will come to light. In the 1950s she came into the ownership of Ted ('Chuggy') Downing, who installed new twin 50hp engines in or about 1962. Her present owner, Ian Childs, was working aboard her from 1963–5, when she was long-lining and drifting out of St Ives; and he purchased her in 1973. She is now fitted with a Baudoin 108hp engine.

Tonnage: 13 gross. Length: (keel) 37ft 7in OA 42ft × beam 13ft × depth 6ft.

Shipshape and Bristol fashion, beyond dispute Ocean Pride *lives up to her name.* Ian Childs.

The ex-German 70ft launch
Victorine *at Lelant.*

Launch *Victorine* (Afloat and working)

Privately owned at Hayle and usually berthed at Lelant Quay is this smart 70-foot launch of German origin. We have been unable to discover her history or present ownership, but the Harbour office have her noted as a World War II German torpedo boat though her build suggests she was more probably designed for inshore patrol work.

Driver *Maid Miriam* (Afloat and working)

A 34-foot pilchard driver, and the only example still afloat. She was built in 1888 so is an old lady indeed. Currently in use as a houseboat and berthed in Penpol Greek, South Quay, she is now for sale. Hull maintenance has been neglected and it would be costly to restore her to seaworthy condition.

River Gannel

The slight remains of the two *Adas* are covered every high water. So must be reached on foot during the lower half of a tide, from either Newquay or Crantock.

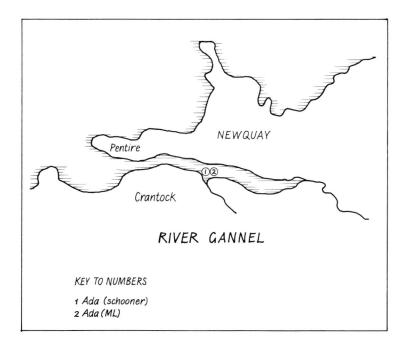

River Gannel (West Bank)

Schooner *Ada* SW 798609

The ebbing tide reduces the River Gannel to a narrow stream, so that one may walk to the last resting-place of the *Ada* over the clean firm sands for most of the time. When the tide rises, cross the river from Newquay by George Northey's Fernpit ferry, and turn left along the footpath which skirts the low cliff at Crantock. High water will not serve, as the *Ada*'s remains are then covered, except for the head of her sternpost.

Built by Peet of Ulverston, Lancashire, in 1876, the *Ada* was a graceful two-masted wood tops'l schooner, classified A1 at Lloyds for most of her life. For many years she was in the coal and china clay trades, and her owner after the turn of the century is recorded as C Isaac. R Salt was her master prior to the Great War, which she came through unscathed.

The incident which brought her nearest to disaster came on March 20 1926, when laden with coal for Truro, and possibly taking the inshore channel past Cape Cornwall, she went ashore on the dreaded Brisons. With the assistance

Ada at Newquay: close-up of figurehead. The Gallery of Old Newquay.

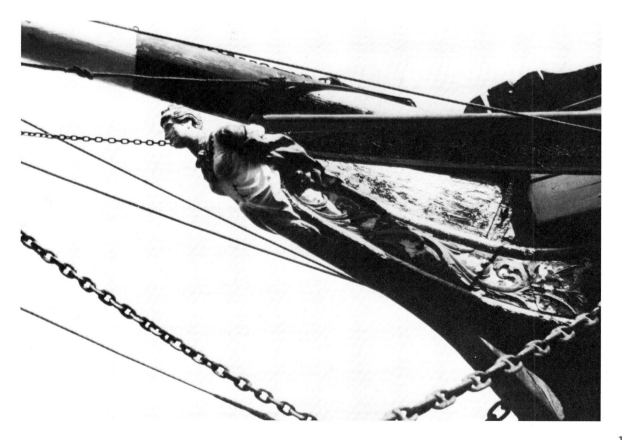

Funeral pyre no 2. Ada ablaze in the Gannel, 1954. Her successor, eventually to suffer the same fate, is on the left. The Gallery of Old Newquay.

of the Sennen lifeboat, the *Ada* refloated and was escorted safely into Newlyn, despite a severe leak.

In 1928, under owner/skipper Thomas A Reed, she arrived at Newquay from Falmouth, moored in the Gannel, and was put up for sale. (It is said that Tom Reed brought *Ada* to the Gannel to prove the river was a navigable channel at a time when a scheme for a bridge was under consideration).

A Mr Ray Bullock acquired her and she was converted to a house boat. With her pleasing lines and painted ports she became a familiar sight at Newquay until after World War II. Part of the interior was laid out as a curio Museum. During this time she was sold again, to Mr HH Thatcher. He was owner when she caught fire in unexplained circumstances and her accommodation was largely gutted. She was partly repaired, but hulked in 1948, becoming then a somewhat dangerous play-ground for children. In the interests of safety her masts were cut down 20 feet by Mr George Northey in 1950; but her owner later decided on more extreme measures, and set fire to her. This time she burned down to her floors.

Her remains have now sunk deep into the sand, but her sternpost is still standing and on my visit her forefoot, apron and part of her stem were recognisable at the other end of her keel. She was partly constructed with iron bolts, and if you go armed with a shovel and some energy it is not difficult to lay bare some of the keelson for examination.

There is a beautiful photograph of *Ada* on page 124 in Basil Greenhill's *A Victorian Maritime Album*, while other photographs are obtainable from the Gallery of Old Newquay, in Springfield Road. Her figurehead has been preserved in Trenence Cottages Museum.

Official number: 70484. Signal letters, HSMK. Tonnage: 133 gross, 95 net. Length: 88·6ft × beam 22·3ft × depth in hold 11·5ft. Moulded depth 11ft 10in. Freeboard: 1ft 6½in. Port of registry: Barrow.

Ex-ML *Ada* (2)   SW 798608

When the schooner *Ada* was hulked in 1948, the owner, Mr HH Thatcher, moved home to an ex-Royal Navy motor launch, many of which had come on to the market with the end of the hostilities. The new houseboat was likewise named *Ada* and moored at a short distance from the hulk.

This launch had been one of three high-speed boats which operated across the North Sea to Norway; so her short life had not been without interest and incident. More than this we have been unable to discover, but we assume she was one of the No 344 experimental class, with stepped hulls, built in 1943. These were designed as MTBs, were twin-screw, powered by 1200bhp Thornycroft engines, and capable of 40 knots. However we cannot be sure that this is the correct identification.

What is certain is that *Ada* passed to the ownership of Mr Thatcher's stepson, Mr P Crantock; and that when her

After the first conflagration and before the second Ada II *lies in the Gannel at low water while part of the buried keel of the burnt-out* Ada I *projects from the sand beyond the bush in the foreground.*

condition deteriorated (it is said that she had broken her back) so that repair was not economic, he set her on fire in true *Ada* tradition and she was completely gutted. The good folk of Newquay could be forgiven for raising their eyebrows. Funeral pyres in the Gannel were becoming a habit! The slender remains of this second *Ada* can still be seen a few yards to the south of her predecessor.

River Camel

The only ship-remains in the River Camel which can still be described as hulks are in Cant Cove. Boats can be hired at Padstow but the time of the tide needs to be judged carefully as a boat will be a liability at low water, and two of the hulks are covered before high water.

By car from Wadebridge, take the B 3314, turning left after Gutt Bridge into the minor road to Rock. A mile and a half later the only left-hand turn will bring you to Court Farm. Here permission must be obtained to leave the car and use the footpath through private land to the cove.

There are three hulks: the identity of one is certain; the identity of the other two is slightly doubtful, but we have indicated the strong probability in each case.

River Camel
(Cant Cove North Bank)

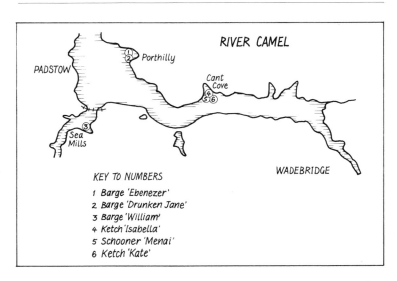

RIVER CAMEL

PADSTOW

Porthilly

Cant Cove

Sea Mills

WADEBRIDGE

KEY TO NUMBERS

1 Barge 'Ebenezer'
2 Barge 'Drunken Jane'
3 Barge 'William'
4 Ketch 'Isabella'
5 Schooner 'Menai'
6 Ketch 'Kate'

Ketch *Isabella*

SW 953747

Access to *Isabella*, *Kate*, and *Menai* is better undertaken by land than by river, but is via a private footpath through Cant Farm, so permission must be sought first. The *Isabella* lies nearest to the point where the footpath reaches the shore of the cove; and access is easy enough for two hours either side of low water.

On our first visit we were fortunate to have the company of the farm manager's delightful children, Philip and Maria Jago, who escorted us on board the *Isabella* and presented us with two shorn-off fastening bolts from the wreck, as souvenirs. Fragments lie in profusion on the sand around her – hawse pipes, chainplates, and rotting timbers. Standing up prominently from the kelson is a heavy steel deck-stanchion which looks to have been not original, but added at some later date to stiffen the vessel at that point. A heavy spar lies athwartships, and remains of the roller-reefing gear. Philip and Maria were not the first children to whom the *Isabella* has played host; for a lady still living in the district remembers how, as a young girl, she used to play on the deck of *Isabella* when the vessel was first abandoned in Cant Cove nearly 40 years ago.

Built at Freckleton, Lancashire, in 1872, this ketch had a reputation in her day for being a fast sailer. In the 'twen-

Children's playground. The Isabella *renders her last service in Cant Cove.* Martin Langley.

ties her owner and manager was Albert Beard of Glouces-ter, who had her fitted with an auxiliary engine in 1925. An unusual feature of *Isabella* was her fidded mizzen top-mast. She was originally designed with schooner rig, and was possibly converted to a ketch when the engine was installed. In her latter years she was owned by a Captain R Orchard, and chiefly employed in transporting stone from Points Quarry. She was registered first at Preston, later at Gloucester.

Official number: 62772. Tonnage: 91 gross, 71 net.
Length: 81·6ft × beam 2·0ft × depth in hold 9·2ft.
Engine: 26bhp.

Schooner *Menai* SW 953746

Walking down the cornfield footpath from Cant Farm, the *Menai* (as we think probable) is the first of the hulks to come into view, as one nears the gate and from under the trees the water of the Cove can be seen below. Only her sternpost, keel and bilge timbers are intact, for every incoming tide covers her, and the alternate immersion and exposure by thousands of tides have hastened her decay. Access is difficult because a boat cannot be brought close until she is awash, and the mud is an effective deterrent to approach from the shore. She lies in the middle of the cove, between the *Kate* and the *Isabella*.

The *Menai* was built originally as a tops'l schooner at Port Dinorwic, midway along the Menai Strait, in 1858. First owned and registered at Caernarvon, she was prematurely written off in 1896, the registrar recording: 'Stranded 11th April 1896, in the Sound of Mull – certificate lost with the vessel. Registry closed 29th April, 1896'. The *Menai* however 'did a phoenix' on the registrar, for some-one got her off and refitted her, and she was thereafter based at Belfast. The Mercantile Navy List records Wm Symington of Belfast as her managing owner.

Len Williams of Padstow remembers helping to recaulk the *Menai* when serving his shipyard apprenticeship. 'She was quite a large ship', he recalls 'and she had a heavy bow'. About 1926/7 she suffered a second stranding at Chapel Bar, Padstow, in bad weather, and was abandoned as a wreck. Again however she was reprieved – this time being refloated by local seamen and thereafter used as a coal hulk. Somehow she missed mention in Clive Carter's *Cornish Shipwrecks, North Coast*.

By 1929 she had disappeared from the Mercantile Navy List. Bill Lindsay of Padstow recalls the *Menai* being dis-masted in the harbour, and her spars and fittings sold by public auction. Having been stripped, it appears the *Menai* was towed up to Cant Cove and abandoned. Mr Fuller, former Harbourmaster at Padstow, told us he remembered seeing her there when he helped to tow in the *Kate*, about 1937.

We cannot be completely certain that this wreck is the *Menai*, in spite of the probabilities, but there is not much room for doubt. One local skipper thought it was a former Thames barge, but the appearance of the remains is against this. Another possibility is the *Hopewell* (qv) but *Hopewell* was a much smaller vessel.

Official number: 20657. Tonnage: 95·66 gross, 76 net.
Length: 79·8ft × beam 20·4ft × depth in hold 10·7ft.

Ketch *Kate* SW 954747

The hulk which we believe to be that of the ketch *Kate* lies close under the east bank of Cant Cove, and can be reached by boat at high water, or on foot by skirting the cove. A direct approach from the footpath gate across the mud is not recommended. Representatives of the North Devon Maritime Museum who salvaged the vessel's windlass crosshead some years ago, approached via the foreshore from the next creek.

The *Kate* was built at Waterford, Ireland, in 1863, and registered there until re-registered at Gloucester on April 29, 1899. In later years she joined the Davis & Stephens fleet at Plymouth, and the Mercantile Navy List for 1929 recorded her owner and manager as Wm H Stephens of Woolster Street. Early in 1936 she stranded whilst entering Padstow and became a constructive total loss, her registration being cancelled on February 28. This ended her commercial life but her hulk, brought later into harbour by longshoremen, was converted to a houseboat.

Before long she had been abandoned and the harbour-

Cant Cove hulks Menai, Kate *and* Hopewell.

The ketch Kate *of Gloucester. Harbourmaster Fuller of Padstow remembers her final trip to Cant Cove.* Cdr H Oliver Hill.

master had her towed to Cant Cove, which had become the graveyard for old ships on the River Camel. Former Padstow Harbourmaster Mr AA Fuller remembers, as a young man, assisting in the operation, and seeing the *Menai* already there, as they made the *Kate* secure in her last resting-place.

We repeat that our identification of this hulk could be mistaken, but after lengthy research we are fairly satisfied that we are right. Those who wish to pursue the matter further, should consider the possibilities of *Menai*, *Hopewell*, or another of the four other *Kates* of approximately the same size which were contemporaneously in Home Waters.

Offical number: 45357. Tonnage: 80·24 gross, 64·10 net. Length: 74·3ft × beam 18·3ft × depth in hold 10·0ft.

Other remains in the Camel

Although we have seen at Cant Cove only the three vessels just described, in fact the remains of a fourth must be there, perhaps exposed only at low water springs, or when a strong tide scours the mud that may be covering her. This is the – *Hopewell*, a ketch of 47 tons net, built as a smack-rigged sloop at Northam in 1863 – first owned at Southampton, later registered at Guernsey, but managed by Albert Westcott of Plymouth. The 1925 Mercantile Navy List records her owner as David W Davies of Ponybryn, Wadebridge. She ended her working days at Padstow, where she was cut down to a barge, and employed carrying stone from Stepper Point quarry to Rock, her owners being the quarry firm.

At Porthilly Cove, Rock, may be found slight remains of two sailing barges, *Ebenezer* and *Drunken Jane*, which were both owned by Bray and Parkly, local corn merchants, and when time-expired were left to rot, at SW 936755. Of the *Ebenezer* we have not details. As to *Drunken Jane*, the name gives rise to speculation as to the identity of the good lady commemorated in this way. The skipper's mother-in-law, perhaps? A small sailing barge with bluff bows but pointed stern. She was ketch-rigged, had no bowsprit, and was steered by tiller. Some years ago the old wooden smack *Genista* was brought to Porthilly Cove and burned on the beach, but we have not seen her remains.

At Sea Mills, in St Issey creek, are slight remains of the *William*, of Fowey. She was last used to bring gravel from Wadebridge when the dock wall at Padstow was built in 1933.

River Torridge

The two main groups of hulks are to be found (a) on the beach immediately north of Appledore Shipyard and (b) on the Northam shore, north of Cleeve Houses. There is no public access to the former, except by hired boat from Appledore, unless permission is sought at the shipyard entrance. To reach the Northam shore wrecks, take the picturesque footpath from Cleeve Houses along the cliff towards Appledore. A track leads down from the cliff path to a cove just north of the hulks.

The remains of *Goldseeker* and *Shamrock* on Skern Sands are only accessible at low water.

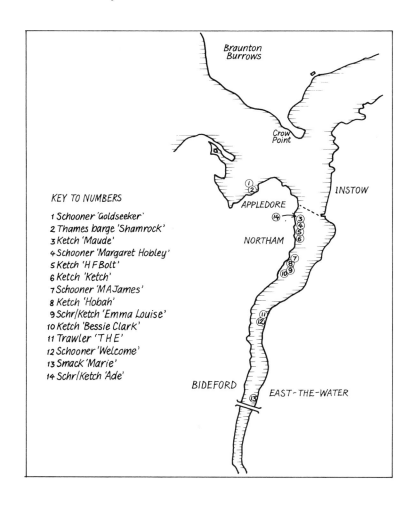

KEY TO NUMBERS

1 Schooner 'Goldseeker'
2 Thames barge 'Shamrock'
3 Ketch 'Maude'
4 Schooner 'Margaret Hobley'
5 Ketch 'H F Bolt'
6 Ketch 'Ketch'
7 Schooner 'M A James'
8 Ketch 'Hobah'
9 Schr/Ketch 'Emma Louise'
10 Ketch 'Bessie Clark'
11 Trawler 'T H E'
12 Schooner 'Welcome'
13 Smack 'Marie'
14 Schr/Ketch 'Ade'

Taking her time to die. Goldseeker *abandoned in the mud at Appledore.* April Whittaker.

Schooner *Goldseeker*   SS 45708

The remains of the schooner *Goldseeker*, with rudder still in position, lie on Skern sands near J Hinks & Son's shipyard, about 100 yards from high water mark. From west Appledore, drive south along the Diddywell road – from which the hulk can be seen – and park near Hinks' yard. Alternatively walk from Appledore lifeboat house past the ruins of the a lime kiln. Skern Sands are reasonably firm, and it is possible to walk out and inspect the ship at low water springs.

The *Goldseeker* was built in 1873 by Qualtrough's at Douglas, IOM, as a two-masted tops'l schooner, and Douglas was her original port of registry. In earlier years her owner was Froude Hill of Bridgwater, although she was managed by John Tyrell of Cardiff. In 1928 her yards were sent down and she was converted to an auxiliary-engined fore-and-after. Her owner/skipper was then William J Caren of Annalong, Co Down. Prior to World War II she was acquired and run by Sir Oswald (Blackshirt) Mosley and partners for some months. *Goldseeker* was not requisitioned during the war, and ran cargoes between Avonmouth, Swansea and Barry. It is believed that her mainmast was removed shortly before the end of her trading days. On withdrawal she was laid up by Bristol Bridge where she lay for a long time. Finally she was purchased by the Harris (shipyard) family for her spares and fittings, and abandoned where her remains still lie – keel, kelson and some bilge timbers, stem, sternpost and rudder.

Official number: 67283. Tonnage: 63 gross, 57 net.
Length: 76ft × beam 21·6ft × depth 9·5ft. Aux engine 30bhp.

The schooner Goldseeker *in Queen's Dock, Glasgow with the ketch Marie Celine.* Dan McDonald of Glasgow.

Thames Barge *Shamrock* SS 458308

The little that remains of this Thames sprits'l barge is to be found on the west beach at Appledore near the ruined lime-kiln mentioned above. A small portion of *Shamrock*'s stern, with a few square feet of her flat bottom, and the end of her iron keel against the foot of her sternpost, will be seen close to the rocks. A few yards away, in the direction of the hulk of the *Goldseeker* lies her much-damaged rudder, heavily encrusted, and swathed in seaweed, for it is covered by every incoming tide.

The *Shamrock* was built at Milton-next-Sittingbourne by White's in 1899. She was virtually a sister ship to the *Beatrice Maud* – still in existence – whose measurements are 88·1ft × 21·2ft × 7·1ft. Most of White's coasters kept fairly consistent dimensions. Her owner and manager in 1929 is recorded as Horace Shrubsall of Tunnel Wharf, East Greenwich. *Shamrock* was not a strong barge, although she had been in the coastal trade until 1939 and on occasions had worked as far north as the Tees. Early in World War II she was damaged in collision, and when repaired was fitted with a Kelvin diesel motor. About 1943 she went to the Bristol Channel for war service, and the fates decreed that she would not return to the East Coast again. Her master then was the late Frank Ellis, and I am indebted to Bob Childs of the Society for Sprits'l Barge Research for the following anecdote.

'Frank Ellis told me an amusing tale about his war service in the Bristol Channel. It would seem he became well-acquainted with a lady in the area, and when the time came for home leave instructed his agents NOT to forward any mail to his home address at Faversham. The first morning that he was home his wife told him to "have a good lay in" whilst she got up and made the tea. Alas, as his wife was proceeding upstairs the postman popped a letter through the front door. On reaching the bedroom his dear wife happened to sniff the envelope . . . and smelt face powder. Poor Frank got the contents of the teapot over him after his wife read the opening message . . . "to my darling sailor". Frank had a very rough leave and was glad to go back to *Shamrock*! Truly, "best-laid plans o' mice and men gang aft agley".'

Her war service over, the *Shamrock* was sold to Barnstaple owners for their local sand trade, but was not long in their service. Captain William Slade of Bideford explained to us: 'In these waters barges need a rounded chine as they continually have to take the ground. There are few places where craft with an absolutely flat bottom can lie for long without damage'. Thus the *Shamrock* was put ashore at West Appledore and cut up. Her registry entry was cancelled in 1947.

Official number: 104943. Tonnage: 69 net.

Ketch *Maude*

SS 465298

Today the tide washes in and out of the *Maude*'s broken hull, hastening her ultimate destruction. Derelict ships can last a long time if immersed in deep water, or – vandals apart – if high and dry. But when left at the water's edge, alternately saturated by incoming tides and dried by sun or wind, rotting is hastened and their days are numbered. The *Maude*, like her three companions on Shipyard Beach, is in such a case. Yet, even in her dereliction, she has grace of line and looks a thoroughbred.

She was built at Widnes on the Mersey in 1869, and registered at Bideford. In her early years she belonged to Joseph Knight of Gloucester, who also owned a ketch named *Emu*. Knight was coal exporter from Lydney to the south of Ireland, and the *Maude* was employed on this run for some years. Thomas Knight became her owner/skipper after the turn of the century. She was next sold to Jack Stoneman of Appledore who re-decked her, ran her for a short while and then sold her to Braunton where she was given an auxiliary engine. Built as a tops'l schooner her yards were later sent down and she was re-rigged as a ketch, but we have no date for conversion, which may have been when the engine was installed – 1930 or later. Knights

The ketch Maude *with the forlorn remains, presumably, of her ship's boat.* April Whittaker.

(photographers) of Barnstaple sell postcards depicting *Maude* with two other ketches at Rolle Quay in the 1930s. The photo shows clearly her semi-elliptical stern and 'out-of-doors' rudder. By 1939 *Maude* was an old vessel and the Government did not requisition her for war service.

Official number: 62010. Tonnage: 54 net.

Ketch *HF Bolt* SS 465298

The remains of this old and once well-known ketch lie outermost of the cluster of hulks on the Shipyard beach. Those who wish to pay their respects must go within three hours either side of low water when the remains are uncovered. This vessel is quite fully documented in WJ Slade's *Westcountry Coasting Ketches* (Conway Maritime Press 1974), which also includes a scale drawing.

HF Bolt was built in 1876 by John Samson of Bideford, which was her port of registry, and her sails were by J Popham of Appledore. Capt Bolt, a deep-water master mariner, was her first owner, and he named the ship after his two daughters Harriett and Florence. In her early days she was in the Newfoundland fish trade, and carried salted cod back to Britain. It is also believed that she made a number of voyages to the north of Spain, bringing back cargoes of nuts. Among her distinctive features were higher-than-average bulwarks, and tiller steering which was not replaced, as in most of the ketches, by a helm wheel. She was however converted to roller reefing on both main and mizzen masts. Captain WK Slade says 'She had the reputation latterly of not being a very good seaboat, but she was not slow in sailing'. In her latter years she was commanded by Capt Wm Fishwick, who had a reputation as a gardener; and on his retirement by his ex-policeman son-in-law, who worked her principally on short runs in the Bristol Channel. She was withdrawn from trade some years before World War II and laid up here, her final resting place, soon becoming tidal.

Her end was hastened by an accident. At the end of the war a number of steel landing barges were laid up close to her. In 1945 one of these dragged her moorings, and in grounding on the ebb tide over-rode the sunken *HF Bolt*, split her open, and crushed her. It was a rather undignified demise for a hard-worked old ship.

Official number: 76713. Tonnage: 68 gross, 51 net, 110 deadweight.
Length: 71·6ft × beam 19·6ft × depth 8·7ft.
Ship's boat: 14·6ft × 5·4ft.

A recent view of the Ketch *showing complete collapse of port side.* April Whitaker.

The Ketch, *mouldering on Shipyard Beach, Appledore.* Edwina Small.

Ketch *Ketch* SS 465298

Possessed of an appropriate but rather unimaginative name, the *Ketch* was built by W Fife & Son at Fairlie on the Firth of Clyde, in 1894. Her port of registry was Ayr. Lloyd's register for 1912–13 records AP Sutherland as her owner, and notes that Capt A Sutherland had been master of her since 1910. Later she was sold to new owners at Portoferry, Co Down, Ireland, who ran her until she was bought by the Jewells of Appledore, about 1923. Captain 'Tommy' Jewell, retired in Appledore, told us: 'I was mate to my father then. We fetched the *Ketch* from Pembroke where she had called to land a cargo of potatoes from Ireland. When we got her back at Appledore we fitted her with a large engine, and ran her for about seven years. She had a Kelvin motor when we bought her, but it was underpowered for the job'. About 1930 Jewells sold the *Ketch* to John Beaza and a Devon Farmer's Syndicate, who ran her with market garden produce between Bideford and Avonmouth. Later she appears in Lloyd's Register as owned by AR Hamlyn of Bristol. The *Ketch* had been well maintained and was requisitioned for balloon-barrage service in World War II, being stationed at Falmouth. As long as such vessels could stay afloat and wind a balloon, their maintenance was largely neglected. Consequently a foul bottom soon developed, and deterioration of the hull followed. As with many other of these ships, the *Ketch* was returned after hostilities in such a condition that repair was uneconomic.

She was run ashore where she lies today, the southernmost of the group, nearest to the Appledore shipyard's main dock. For'ard her port side has been partly cut away, and her stern has split open, but one of her deck beams is still in position.

Official number: 99732. Tonnage: 70 gross, 56 net.
Length: 69 ft × beam 19·7ft × depth 9·2ft.

Schooner *MA James* SS 465294

The remains of this fine old schooner are the northernmost of the four hulks below the cliff path from Bideford to Appledore. She was the largest of the vessels in this group and is still the most complete hull, despite the depredations of timber hunters. The *MA James* is well documented by Captain WJ Slade of Bideford in his book *Out of Appledore*. He was her master in the 'twenties, and it is to meeting him personally and reading what he has written that we are mainly indebted for the information given here.

Built in 1900 at Portmadoc for the North Atlantic trade to Newfoundland, 'the *MA James* was' says Captain Slade, 'typical of the great series of merchant schooners built at Portmadoc between 1890 and 1913, which in many ways represented the finest development of the British schooner.' Owned for the first 17 years by John Jones of Portmadoc, and registered initially at Carnarvon, she then

The M.A. James *at Mousehole in 1922.* Cdr H Oliver Hill.

Time, tide and wood plunderers have done their worst: the M.A. James *today on the banks of the Torridge.* April Whittaker.

changed hands twice, being operated by the Plymouth Co-operative Society from 1919–1930.

It was in 1930 that she was bought at Plymouth by Capt WJ Slade for £750; the last vessel to join the Slade fleet, she remained with them for the rest of her seagoing life. She was in a poor state of maintenance when taken over, and £1195 had to be spent on refitting her and installing a 70hp auxiliary engine. She had a reputation for being slow, but Capt Slade's father admired her lines and expressed his opinion that she would sail well. He was right, and the undeserved reputation must have been due to indifferent handling. In fact, the *MA James* held an unofficial record for the fastest schooner passage from Tremadoc Bay to Harburg, Germany. The Slades knew their tides, a pre-requisite for successful sail trading in Home Waters; and moreover were supreme ship handlers. In their hands the *MA James* soon made nonsense of her former reputation, proving as fast as they could wish, and a good money-earner. Until they sealed her to their satisfaction, the *MA James* made quite a lot of water, and Capt Slade recalled how, after an exhausting day when the pumps had to be worked every half hour, he had to spend nearly two hours of what should have been his watch below, perched on the tops'l yard, reeving off a new fore-brace on a cold dark night with a sea running. During the 1930s Capt WJ Slade's brother, George Slade, was skipper of the *MA James*.

Came World War II, and the *MA James* was requisitioned for balloon-barrage service. The same sad story of neglect and incompetent maintenance as applied to many other commandeered vessels was repeated. Hostilities ended, the *MA James* returned to Appledore under her own power and was moored off the shipyard pending survey. The survey showed that £5000 worth of repairs was necessary. Certainly there was at least a moral obligation on the Government to carry out this work. The ship's market value was £4000 and the Government, regarding the ship as CTL (Constructive Total Loss) paid this and also handed over the vessel. She was sold to Harris's shipyard for £700. They used her in a lifting operation to recover a fallen 80-ton crane from the river, sold her engine, stripped her, and put her ashore where she lies today. Captain WJ Slade describes her as 'one of the finest and best built schooners that had sailed the Atlantic Ocean and the Mediterranean for many years'.

Official number: 109732. Tonnage: 97 net.
Length: 89·6ft × beam 22·7ft × depth 10·6ft.
Latterly registered at Plymouth.

Ketch *Hobah*   SS 465294

This wooden ketch was built 1878/9 on the beach at Trellew Creek, Mylor, Cornwall; a 'one-off job' by shipwright Thomas Gray, with two assistants. She proved to be quite

Hobah, *showing her main topmast raked forward.* Cdr H Oliver Hill.

a fast vessel. Thomas Gray and Philip Quenault were the first owners, Quenault sailing as Master. In these early days, according to late Appledore tradition, she made a voyage to the Mediterranean with granite blocks for harbour construction. In 1908 she was acquired by DA Hyett and C Lamey of Appledore. During refit that year the foc'sle was fitted up with bunks. For about 30 years she was skippered by Captain William Lamey, who latterly owned her entirely. A 30bhp Gardner engine fitted in 1911 had proved inadequate, so her rig was never cut down.

One of her distinctive features was her main topmast, which was raked well for'ard, as it was found that her main-mast had been stepped too far aft. Captain W Slade has recorded in *Westcountry Coasting Ketches* that *Hobah* was the last ship to discharge a cargo at Newquay, in 1922; and the last to discharge a beach cargo at Porth Luney, South Cornwall in 1937. She continued to make a living until the second year of World War II, making her last voyage (Plymouth to Appledore with coal) in June 1940. Her motor broke down and she was long overdue when she berthed. Hull and engine were alike worn out, and she was laid up in the Torridge where her keel and bilge timbers can still be seen. Eight years later the schooner *MA James* was put ashore at the same place and settled across the *Hobah*'s bow. Evidently this old ketch was one of many which inspired affection in those who took them to sea. The following is reproduced, with permission, from Basil Greenhill's *The Merchant Schooners* Volume 1:

Captain Lamey spoke of his father, Charles Lamey, in these words: 'Often, towards the end of his life, after we had brought the *Hobah* into Appledore Quay he would go down there after the day's work and sit watching her. I would say to him, 'What are you doing, father? 'Tis late now and you had best be coming home'', and he would say to me "I'm just looking at the *Hobah*, son, I'm just looking at the *Hobah*". At the time I thought it was strange that anyone should feel that way about a ship, but I found myself doing the same thing before the end of my time with her'.

The *Hobah* is perhaps the best documented of all North Devon ketches. Plans of her, and much of her history, appear in Basil Greenhill's *The Merchant Schooners*. Two models of her, both by Captain T Jewell of Appledore, are in existence. One is on display in the National Maritime Museum, along with relics of the ship: the other is privately owned by relatives of Captain Lamey's son, who died in 1978.

Official number: 81154. Tonnage: 76 gross, 56 net, 110 deadweight. Length: 78·6ft × beam 19·9ft × depth 9·0ft. Classified A1 at Lloyd's.

A photo Captain Lamey and his son would not have wished to see, neglected but still recognisable here, no-one sits and looks at Hobah *today.*

Sadly resembling a corner of Steptoe's yard, the Emma Louise *and her engine casing beside the Torridge.* Martin Langley.

Ketch *Emma Louise*   SS 465294

The *Emma Louise* is in the middle of the group of hulks at Northam, immediately south of the *MA James*. Her back is broken and she is little more than a jumble of distorted timbers, unrecognisable as the once graceful ketch which was built by W Westcott of Barnstaple in 1881.

Her early employment was from Braunton and Appledore in the Bristol Channel and across the St George's Channel to southern Irish ports, with general cargoes. From 1904 till the Great War she was skippered by Philip Hutchings, with Tim McCarthy as Mate. When hostilities broke out they were both called up, being Naval reservists. Her owner then was JH Gorvin, After the war she was acquired by the Rawle family of Minehead, and traded from this Somerset port for some years. Later she went to Aberdeen, where an auxiliary engine was fitted. From there she was brought back to Appledore by the Guard family. *Emma Louise* was a typical product of Westcott's yard, with a sharp, almost hollow, forefoot, and a delicate carving on her stemhead, lined out in colour. When the vessel was finally laid up and stripped, the ornamentation was carefully preserved and Captain Slade states that it is still in existence.

Emma Louise was the only ketch trading out of Appledore with a steel deckhouse over her engine compartment; its rusted, broken remains still lie in her stern.

Official number: 84475. Tonnage: 72 gross, 66 net.
Length: 75·4ft × beam 19·8ft × depth 8·3ft. Port of Registry: Barnstaple. Classified A1 at Lloyd's.

Ketch *Bessie Clark*   SS 465294

The shattered remains of this wooden ketch lie southernmost of the group of hulks at this point. At only 44 tons she was the smallest of the four, but she had her own claim to distinction. We have been told, on good authority, that she was originally converted from a steamer, but can find no documentary evidence for this. However, it cannot be denied that she was certainly the first of the Bristol Channel ketches to have an auxiliary engine, which was installed 1909.

The *Bessie Clark* was completed in 1881 by HM Restarick of East-the-Water, Bideford, a yard which closed five years later. She was registered in Barnstaple, and owned for most of her life by George and Henry Clark of Braunton. George Clark had previously owned and sailed the smack *Bessie Gould* named after his fiancee. When he married this young lady, he sold the *Bessie Gould* and ordered the *Bessie Clark* from Restaricks. As far as we can ascertain, she was built new and was not a conversion. Like other Braunton men who owned rented vegetable plots and liked to put in work on them if windbound in a nearby port, Capt George Clark habitually kept a bicycle in the *Bessie Clark* which, if at anchor on moorings, he would take ashore with him in the ship's boat. Michael Bouquet records in *Westcountry Sail* (1971) that this caused some amusement among the seafarers at Appledore: 'They Bra'nton men take their bikes to say with 'en'.'

We have not been able to discover whether the *Bessie Clark* was requisitioned in World War II: by then she would have been 58 years old. Today little of the ship survives. Stem and sternpost have gone, ribs sag forlornly and askew, and keelbolts project prominently where much of her kelson has been cut away.

Official number: 84471. Tonnage: 46 gross, 40 net.
Length: 59·1ft × beam 18·2ft × depth 7·5ft. Engine 12 hp.

Schooner *Margaret Hobley*   SS 465298

Built as a two-masted tops'l schooner at Pembroke Dock in 1868, the *Margaret Hobley*'s port of registry was London. She was owned originally by Thomas Hobley of Carnarvon and later by William Postlewaite of Millom. An auxiliary

A fine picture of the Margaret Hobley *dried out and waiting for the tide.*

Margaret Hobley *under sail in the Bristol Channel*. Tom Slade of Appledore.

engine of 80hp was installed in 1921, and either at this time or soon after she was converted to a three-masted fore-and-aft schooner. In 1922 she was sold by the Hook Shipping Company to William Quance of the Slade family for £1,200, and was commanded by Captain Tom Slade for 25 years. During this period she was fitted with an iron 'rider' kelson, above the wood kelson proper, to stiffen her.

In World War II the *Margaret Hobley* was requisitioned for balloon-barrage service, and moored at Falmouth. Little more was asked of balloon-barrage vessels than the ability to stay afloat, and as long as they could do so no maintenance was carried out on their hulls. *Margaret Hobley* was returned in a dilapidated state to her owners after hostilities, and not refitted. She was put ashore where she lies today and de-registered in 1948.

It is said locally that a bulldozer was driven through her remains some years ago, when work was proceeding on the Appledore shipyard; certainly her hull has been severed. She is easily identified as the middle-positioned of the four hulks on Shipyard beach. When the tide is up her midships is covered, and her bow, split open, rises mutely from the water.

Official number: 55374. Tonnage: 119 gross, 82 net.
Length: 86·6ft × beam 22·2ft × depth 10·8ft. Engine: 80bhp.

Trawler *T.H.E.* SS 459278

The remains of the trawler *T.H.E.* and of the schooner *Welcome* lie only yards apart on Limekiln Beach, between Bideford East-the-Water and Instow on the east bank of the Torridge. The position is easily reached by boat, but those driving over Bideford Bridge turn left on to the A 39 Instow Road, and (where the street lamp-standards end), will find a shallow lay-by on the nearside, where the car may be left. From here a track leads down through the bushes to the goods-only railway line, which must be crossed to reach the river beach.

The trawler's stem and sternpost have bone, but the full length of the keel remains, with some starb'd ribs and planking amidships. Some of the garboard strakes are badly warped, and grass has taken root amid the floors of the port side. The *T.H.E.* was a mule class Brixham trawler and her portmark BM 275. Built in 1908 by Jackman of Brixham for owner/skipper Tom Harris, her name derives from his three daughters, Teresa, Harriet and Edith. Retired Brixham fisherman Ned Widger recalls that at one time the *T.H.E.* had her hull painted grey, but she is in the traditional black in the only photo we have of her, which shows her competing in the mule race at Brixham regatta during the 1920s. Ned Widger remembers compet-

T.H.E. (BM 275) competing in the Mule race, Brixham Regatta. She is second from the left. Author's collection.

ing against her in this event, when he was mate of the *Guess Again*.

Skipper Tom Harris was a notable character: a prominent member of the Salvation Army at Brixham, he was very proud of his uniform, and frequently wore his 'Sally Ann' cap to sea, wind permitting. He was surely the only trawlerman to have done so!

T.H.E. left Brixham in 1937 when she was sold to Captain Pile of Bideford and, according to PM Herbert of Bude, used for trawling in the Bay. In November 1940 she was fitted with an engine and taken up by the Navy to become a patrol vessel in the Lundy area. After the war she was used as houseboat on the Torridge by the pseudonymous author 'Sinbad', who was her last owner.

Official number: 125109. Tonnage: 36 gross, 25·8 net. Length: 61·5ft × beam 17·1ft × depth 7·4ft.

Schooner *Welcome*   SS 459277

Built by P Rawstrone at Freckleton, Lancashire, in 1885 as a three-masted tops'l schooner, the *Welcome* was first registered at Preston, and owned by JLT Armstrong. Later she was owned and registered at Gloucester and converted, like most other West Country coasters, to a fore-and-aft rigged auxiliary. Eventually she was acquired by

Fast aground, the Welcome *exposes her keelson on Limekiln Beach.* Martin Langley.

William Cox, and operated from Appledore. So far as is known, her trading career of over 50 years was without any serious mishap.

In World War II the *Welcome* was requisitioned for balloon barrage work and stationed at Falmouth. After return to her owners, she was laid up in the Torridge for sale, in unseaworthy condition. Here she was bought by John Beara and WJ Slade, who removed everything of value, including the ship's wheel, and sold the hulk for £50 for breaking. Her new pitchpine decks were floated to Bideford and used for the floor of the Rugby Football Club building then under construction.

The *Welcome*'s purchasers did not collect her, and shortly after she was found adrift by the Harbourmaster and put ashore on the Instow bank, where her remains lie today.

Official number: 88713. Tonnage: 119 gross, 93 net, 190 deadweight. Length: 94·0ft × beam 22·4ft × depth 9·6ft.

Lesser fry

About midway between the group of wrecks at Northam and that at Shipyard Beach lies an unpretentious motor barge, the *J. J. R. Pile*, built by Waters of West Appledore in 1925. Her acquisition was considered by the North Devon Maritime Museum Trust *c* 1978, but restoration was found to be beyond their resources. The hull is complete, but tidal. There is also an abandoned motor sand-barge, with white painted gunnel, on the beach at Instow.

Drying her sails the Welcome *at anchor sometime in the 1920s.* NMM.

Gravel Barge *Advance* (Afloat and refitting)

In the summer of 1986 the North Devon Museum Trust announced its intention to buy and restore, subject to satisfactory survey, the gravel barge *Advance*, then moored on the north bank of Torridge at Bideford. The owner was prepared to sell if restoration could be guaranteed. One of the last of North Devon wooden barges, the *Advance* is listed in the International Register of Historic Ships published by the World Ship Trust. The Manpower Services Commission were prepared to assist in the restoration work and Appledore Shipbuilders have promised co-operation. The intention is to carry out the work over a four-year period, giving time to raise the money required.

Tonnage: 20 gross, 12 net. Length: 50·0ft. Built: 1926 by Robert Cock & Sons for the Devon Trading Company.

Built by Date's of Kingsbridge in 1904, the Marie *was registered throughout her career at Salcombe. In the thirties she came often to Plymouth to load maize and during the last war she served as a balloon barrage vessel. Now aground and tidal at Bideford East-the-Water she suffers the indignity of being used as a receptacle for junk but her demolition is probably imminent.* April Whittaker.

River Parrett

The rivers of Somerset are for the most part narrow, steeply-banked, very muddy, subject to extreme ranges of tide, and with few creeks. The Parrett is no exception, and has a tidal bore at spring tides. Such rivers are not ideal resting places for time-expired ships; and a boat is of little use for inspecting such hulks as lie in the Parrett.

Drive to Combwich, parking by the river bank, for the *Trio*, stone barge, and the *Severn*. To see the *Safety*, drive on to Dunball wharf, take the public footpath skirting Bibby's factory, and cross the pasture field. *Trio* and *Safety* are only visible at low water.

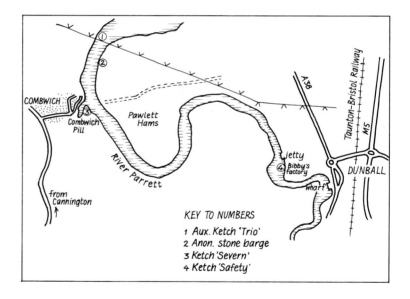

KEY TO NUMBERS

1 Aux. Ketch 'Trio'
2 Anon. stone barge
3 Ketch 'Severn'
4 Ketch 'Safety'

Aux Ketch *Trio*   ST 264434

Half a mile downstream from Combwich where the grid wires cross the river, in the trough of the Parrett and exposed only at low water, is the mastless hull of the motorized ketch *Trio*. Built with the name *Warinula* at Jersey in 1877 as a schooner with topsail and flying t'gallant sail, she was renamed *Margherita* some years later and about the turn of the century came, as *Trio*, into the possession of a the Escott family of Watchet. In 1907 she joined the Slade fleet at Appledore for £225 and was re-rigged as a ketch. Nearly all Appledore ships were manned by naval reservists, and with the outbreak of World War

Trio of Bideford as she would have looked at her commissioning in 1877. NMM.

The ship that fell from Pursey's Mare. The Trio, *Captain Warren's last command, still lies in the Parrett at Combwich.* AV Stone of Watchet.

I they were laid up with no crews. Jack Reece, master of the *Trio*, was one of the first to lose his life in action. The *Trio* was soon at sea again, skippered by one of the Slade brothers. They strengthened the ship by fitting iron stringers from the underside of her beam to the kelson; but when the war ended they sold her to the Salt Union of Gloucester. In 1926 she was bought by Mrs Elizabeth Warren of Bridgwater. Her mainmast was poled off and a 9hp auxiliary engine fitted. Under Captain Joe Warren, the owner's husband, she traded mostly in the Bristol Channel until an accident ended her career six years later.

In 1935 she was proceeding light up the Parrett to Bridgwater to load bricks and tiles. To await the tide at Bridgwater, skipper Warren took her out of Midchannel to put her over 'Pursey's Mare', a level mudbank which was reckoned a safe berth. But there were no markers of any kind, and Capt Warren had unwittingly put his ship on the edge of the bank. When the tide fell, the *Trio* fell over; and when the tide made again, she was swamped, and lay sunk. The crew had escaped safely in her boat, and her principal fittings were salvaged. But the *Trio* herself was doomed. Captain Warren collected the insurance, and retired from the sea.

A visit to the wreck must be timed for low water, preferably springs. Park at the end of the Combwich common and take the riverside path.

Official number: 75264. Tonnage: 63 net.

A Schooner's cargo   ST 308405

Those who have only seen the River Parrett at low water or half-tide may be surprised to learn that about 500 ships, of about 1000-1200 tons dead weight, still come up the Parrett every year. In the days of the merchant schooners and coasting ketches a far greater number of vessels braved the river's serpentine channel and fast-falling tides to reach the quays at Combwich, Dunball, and Bridgwater Docks. Among these was the schooner *Happy Harry* (115 tons) of Whitehaven, built at Duddon in 1894 and owned by Job Tyrrell of Arklow. She went aground in the 'belly' of the Parrett at Dunball in 1932 when sailing for Ireland. Her cargo of bricks and slate were frantically dumped in the river, and the ship refloated. But remains of that dumped cargo can still be seen at low water springs.

Ketch *Severn*   ST 261422

This old wooden ketch is reverting to nature in Combwich Pill, a once busy little harbour on the south bank, reached by a minor road leaving the A39 at Cannington. The remains of the *Severn* lie in the innermost part of the harbour. Her triple sternpost, with rudder still on its pintles,

The Severn *in Combwich Pill.*

stands erect from the keel which has sunk into the mud. Her kelson and floors are breaking up. Built at Bridgwater in 1867, the *Severn* spent her working life in the Bristol Channel. In the late 'twenties her skipper was Cecil Bowerman, and she was owned by the Somerset Trading Company.

Official number: 56363. Tonnage: 75 net.

Unnamed Barge   ST 265433

This large but 'dumb' barge was last used as a stone-carrier during the building of the Shell-Mex-BP oil terminal at Walpole. Registered at Gloucester she was towed by a Bridgwater tug after loading from lorries at a local quarry The Harbourmaster authorised her abandonment here, by the Pawlett Hams. The wreck is only visible at low water. Drive to the end of the Hams – through five gates! On reaching the bank walk half a mile round the bend of the river, downstream.

Barque *Nornen* ex-*Maipu*   ST 285525

Berrow (near mouth of River Brue)
The coast of Somerset is not rich in hulks or veteran craft, so we felt it admissible here to include the remains of the Norwegian barque *Nornen*, though this is in fact a shipwreck. On Berrow Sands, opposite the church, can be seen her keel, part of the kelson, rib timbers, stern post and some planking. Outer planking only survives in the bilges, but this still has some copper sheathing.

On the night of March 2/3 1897, the *Nornen* bound for Brunswick in ballast, was sheltering in Lundy Roads from hurricane-force winds when her cables parted and she was swept across the Bristol Channel. Heavy seas were breaking on the Berrow flats when she drove ashore, having by then lost all her canvas. The Burnham-on-Sea lifeboat, *The John Godfrey Morris*, was launched at 10am but took $1\frac{1}{2}$ hours, pulling against wind and tide, to reach the barque. Meanwhile the *Nornen*'s master, Capt P Olsen, had got ashore with the help of ropes thrown by people wading into the breakers, but his crew of ten would not follow him, so were brought ashore by the lifeboat.

Over the next few days the *Nornen* was lightened, but attempts to refloat her failed, and on April 2 1897 she was sold as a wreck. Her figurehead (displayed beside the gate of a nearby cottage) and ship's bell have been preserved. For years the wreck was buried and lost to sight but since gales shifted the sands in 1965 has been visible again.

Built Bordeaux 1876 as *Maipu*. Tonnage: 710 gross, 688 net. Length: 154·5ft × beam 31·6ft × depth 20·1ft.

Since uncovered by shifting sands, the Nornen*'s sturdy remains have become a familiar sight to thousands of holidaymakers.* Edwina Small.

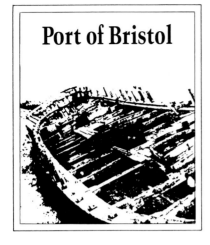

Floating Harbour

SS *Great Britain*   Great Western Drydock

A great deal of information about this famous vessel, both in text and illustration, is readily obtainable from the SS *Great Britain* Trading Company Ltd, Gas Ferry Road, Bristol, and here we shall do no more than record the principal features of the ship and a summary of her history. Built by the Great Western Steamship Company in 1843, in the very dock in which she now lies, the ship was intended for their own transatlantic service and was designed by the great Isambard K Brunel. That design was

One of the many hulks derelict in Sparrow Cove, Falklands, Great Britain *awaits her refloating and long tow back to Britain in 1970.* SS Great Britain Trading Company.

The new life has begun for Great Britain, *now a major tourist attraction in the dock at Bristol where she was built in 1843.* SS Great Britain Trading Company.

revolutionary in many aspects and the *Great Britain* has several claims to fame and a unique place in British shipping history.

She was the first ocean-going ship to have an iron hull, and the first ocean-going ship to be driven by a screw propellor. (Ipso facto she was the first screw steamer to cross the Atlantic). She was the first ship with a double bottom, the first ship with transverse bulkheads, and the first seagoing vessel with wire rigging. In addition to these important innovations she was, at the time of her completion, the largest ship afloat.

As built, the *Great Britain* had a single funnel and six masts for carrying sail, and it is to this original condition that she is now being restored. Her intended service on the Atlantic lasted only 14 months, from July 1845 to September 1846, when she stranded in Dundrum Bay, Ireland, and could not be refloated for 12 months. The cost of salvage compelled her owners to sell her, and the second phase of her career saw her running between Liverpool and Melbourne, Australia for Gibbs, Bright and Co. In 1851 she was given a new engine and boilers and her external appearance altered by twin funnels and a reduction of her masts to four. The *Great Britain* remained in the Australian service for 24 years, but was again altered, in 1853, to three masts and in 1857 to a single funnel. During this period she was twice requisitioned for trooping, first from 1855–6 for the Crimean War, and later for the Indian Mutiny, 1857. In 1868 her master, Capt John Greay, was lost overboard in somewhat mysterious circumstances. From 1876–82 the ship was laid up at Birkenhead, for sale.

Antony Gibbs, Sons & Co, a related company, purchased the *Great Britain* in 1882. They removed her engines and funnel, replaced her passenger accommodation with cargo holds, and used her as a sail freighter (full rigged ship) between South Wales and the Pacific coast of America. On her third such voyage she was strained, her cargo shifted in heavy seas off Cape Horn, and she had to seek shelter in the Falklands Islands. Sold then to the Falkland Islands Company, she was used for 50 years as a floating storeship for coal and wool in Stanley Harbour. In 1937 she was towed to Sparrow Cove, beached and left to decay. Here she lay for 33 years, when it was determined to salvage her if possible and bring her home. Her refloating, lifting on to a submersible pontoon, and subsequent 7000-mile ocean tow to Bristol, in 1970, was made possible by the munifence of British philanthropist Sir Jack Hayward, who defrayed the cost; and was a major salvage triumph of recent times.

Tonnage: 3443 burthen, 1016 net. Length: 322ft × beam 51ft. Original engines 4-cylinder reciprocating 2000ihp. Speed 12 knots.

Hull Trawler *William McCann*
(Afloat and at work)

The William McCann, *former Hull sailing trawler, earning her living in her fishing days, now doing charter work from Bristol City Docks.* Henry Irving.

Last of the Humber sailing trawlers and now over 100 years old, the *William McCann* has had five previous names and since 1980 has borne the name of her maker. McCann was the most prolific of the Humber smack builders, and completed the *City of Edinboro* – as the vessel was first named – in 1884, to the orders of Simpson & Bowman, whose fleet fished the North Sea grounds with trawl and long-line.

The advent of steam trawlers rang the death knell for the smacks, which had disappeared from the Humber by 1900. Many of them found a new lease of life in the less sophisticated fishing ports of Iceland, Norway and the Faroes, the *City of Edinboro* going to Iceland in 1897. Renamed *Frida*, she fished from Iceland till 1913, then from the Faroes till 1943. A change of ownership in 1943 brought a change of name – *Solvasker* – which she carried till 1961 when renamed *Sjoborgin*. In 1980, still working, she was discovered by her present owner/skipper, Henry Irving, who already owned *Venture*, the last of the Humber shrimpers. He persuaded *Sjoborgin*'s owner to sell, brought her back to Hull, renamed her after her builder, and restored her in time for centenary celebrations in 1984.

The *William McCann* is now available for charter anytime, anywhere, at £20 per person per day with all food included, provided there is a minimum of 15 charterers. The foc'sle and fish hold have been gutted and redesigned to provide 20 berths – each with individual wardrobe and locker – a washroom area, and modern galley. One- or two-week cruises are the norm, around the coast of Britain and North Europe in summer, and around the Canary Isles in winter. The charter guests need no previous seagoing experience but are instructed in manning the ship to supplement the trained crew of six. They experience the thrill of sailing a large vessel at speeds up to 10 knots, but the Burmeister Wain diesel engine is used when entering or leaving harbour.

Official number: 88180. Tonnage: 83·42 gross, 47·79 net. Length: 86·0ft (110ft with sprit) × beam 20·0ft. Draught: 10ft 9in.

Steam Tug *Mayflower* (Afloat and at work)

The 32-ton, 63½ft *Mayflower* is the oldest surviving Bristol-built vessel afloat, and except for the 1857 Swedish tug *Fortuna* is probably the oldest still-serviceable tug in the world.

Built by Stothert & Marten of Hotwells in 1861, she was one of the three tugs – the others were *Moss Rose* (1860) and *Violet* (1861) – ordered by the Gloucester & Berkeley Canal Company to augment, and eventually replace, horse towage between Sharpness and Gloucester. *Mayflower* was engined by her builders with a single-cylinder vertical engine, which was replaced in 1899 by a Sissons vertical compound condensing engine, and this she still has today. In 1904 she was dry-docked at Gloucester for replating; and remained in this dock for five years – being refloated and resettled every time the dock was flooded to admit or release other vessels! When she emerged in 1909 it was with a new two-flue coal-fired Scotch boiler, which has never been replaced.

After 1922 her working area was changed to the River Severn above Gloucester, to Stourport and Worcester; and alterations were made to adapt her for this work. Her bulwarks were cut away amidships on either side, and the deck raised a foot (to facilitate work at riverside wharves), while her funnel was hinged and balanced by counterweights (to clear low bridges). It seems that these modifications were soon considered by the *Mayflower*'s crew to be disadvantageous and no doubt it was due to their objections that eventually the bulwarks were restored and the funnel shortened 15 inches to obviate lowering.

The accommodation for the crew of four can best be described as spartan. The steering position was originally shielded from the weather only by a canvas dodger, later by an iron screen. Not until the days of World War II was a wheelhouse provided, and by then the *Mayflower* was 80 years old. The only cabin space was a small foc's'le until the 1920s when a tiny after cabin was provided. When British Waterways took over in 1948 a 'heads' (toilet) was fitted in the foc's'le. Prior to this the crew had 'gone in the coal'. The procedure was to place a shovelful of coal on the boiler room floor, squat over the shovel, then shoot the lot into the furnace. Within seconds an anguished cry of 'You dirty sods!' would be heard from the barge being towed astern.

About 1950 British Waterways modernised the rest of the tug fleet with diesel engines, but *Mayflower* was relegated to reserve tug and retained her steam engine which was overhauled in 1953. She assisted in salvage operations when the M/V *Azurity* crashed into a canal swing-bridge; and in the severe winter of 1962/3 when the canal froze over, *Mayflower* had a last laugh over her diesel sisters, doing most of their towing, because their fuel lines froze and they could not start.

In 1964 she was laid up in Gloucester Docks and miraculously escaped the attentions of vandals and scrap merchants for 15 years. Bristol City Museum & Art Gallery purchased her in April 1981 and a group of volunteers have since been completely renovating the ship and her machinery. She can usually be seen berthed outside the

Industrial Museum. It is intended to steam her occasionally and in 1987 she is scheduled to make a return visit to the canal she served so long.

Official number: 105412. Tonnage: 32 gross, 0 net.
Length: 63·3ft × beam 12ft × depth 7·2ft. Engine 30hp.

Tug *Durdham* (Afloat and at work)

The *Durdham* can usually be found berthed near the Industrial Museum, in which a model of her is on display. She was built to the orders of Kings Tugs Ltd, in 1936 as the *John King*; and though constructed on the lines of a steam tug was fitted with a Polar Diesel engine, later replaced by a Lister Blackstone. All her service was in the port of Bristol, but Kings later sold her to Bristol Commercial Ships who renamed her *Peterleigh*. A second change of name, to *Durdham*, came when she was acquired by Ashmeads who withdrew her in 1972. Built in Charles Hill's yard, she should not be confused with another Bristol-built *Durdham*, a dredger launched in 1930. Today she is the oldest surviving Bristol tug that still sees some commercial use, and is now owned by the Devon & Somerset Shipping Company.

Length: 62·0ft × beam 18·0ft × draught 8·6ft.

Ex-ML *Fairmile B* (Afloat and at work)

Now owned by Mr RG Morley of Bristol, this vessel is the last former-ML still in World War II condition. Built at Hamworthy in the Port of Poole in 1941, she was commissioned on September 1 that year as *ML 293*. Her war service was lively. On March 30 1942 she was damaged in the raid of St Nazaire. Just over two months later she was in action twice in three days; sinking an enemy patrol boat near Etaples on June 4 and landing special service troops at Etaples on June 6 when she damaged a German patrol boat with gunfire. At sea in company with *ML 139*, she was attacked by five German aircraft on July 14 and three of her crew were killed. Shelled by enemy coastal batteries in December that year, *ML 293* suffered damage and four of her crew were lost. In February 1943 she was damaged in an air attack while on patrol with *ML 343*. The last major incident in her war service came in July 1944 when two of her crew died in action off Anzio. Few if any MLs in World War II made a greater contribution, as she had landed commandos in various reconnaisance raids on the French coast, patrolled as a U-boat hunter, and was latterly used for air-sea rescue. She is reported to have once carried King George VI, accompanied by *ML 529*.

Today she is still in use as a Sea Cadet training ship, based in Bristol's floating harbour.

Taking a stern view of the situation. Lochiel *at Bristol.* Martin Langley.

Island Packet *Lochiel* (Afloat and at work)

The former mail packet *Lochiel* is now a floating Inn and restaurant, moored by the Exhibition Centre in St Augustine's Reach, and owned by Courage, the Brewers. Built in 1939 by Denny of Dumbarton for David Macbrayne Ltd, she was employed as a passenger and cargo carrier between the Scottish Islands, and was the fourth ship of that name on the service. The growth of vehicular traffic in the 1960s necessitated modifications to enable her to carry 16 cars, but they had to be craned on and off. In 1970 she was withdrawn and sold to an Isle of Man firm, Norwest Shipping Ltd. Renamed *Norwest Laird*, she ran a service between Douglas and Fleetwood; but this proved unremunerative and she was laid up in Glasson Dock.

Three years later she was bought by Courage (Western) Limited, who restored her original name and spent £200,000 converting her to a well-furnished floating pub and restaurant. Her recommissioning as such coincided with the World Wine Fair in Bristol and was attended by her former Master for 17 years, Captain Donald Macleod of Lochgilphead. With good catering facilities the ship has become a busy lunch spot for city workers and a popular meeting-place at night. On one occasion so many patrons crowded the starb'd rail to watch a firework display that the *Lochiel* had a 15 degree list.

Official number: 5210492. Tons: 577 gross, 205 net.
Length: 190·6ft × beam 32·1ft × depth 7·4ft.
Engines (now removed): twin Paxman diesels, 880bhp.

Ex-RMAS *Freshspring* (Afloat and at work)

It is rare indeed for an RMAS vessel to be preserved in private ownership and put on view to the public, but *Freshspring* is the exception that proves the rule. She was built to Admiralty specification by the Lytham Shipbuilding Company, and launched at St Annes, Lancashire, in 1947. Designed primarily as a fresh-water carrier, she was also equipped for fire-fighting and marine salvage. Most of her working life was spent in Malta, operating from Valetta dockyard. *Freshspring* returned to Britain in 1975 to undergo refit at Portsmouth. She was towed to Greenock the following year by the tug *Advice*, and placed in reserve. 1979 saw her sold out of service to Messrs Burgess and Fox of Bristol where she arrived in January 1980. The original intention to employ her commercially in the work for which she was designed were not however fulfilled, and Mr Burgess, now sole owner, is restoring *Freshspring* to original condition, with the help of a volunteer team of local enthusiasts. Normally berthed outside the Industrial Museum and open to the public at a small charge, the

Once a servant of the Royal Navy, today the Freshspring *is 'at home' to visitors at the Bristol Industrial Museum.* Richard Clammer.

Xenia *on the quayside at Bristol City Docks in 1986. A Sunday morning scene so no restoration activity is in progress.* Martin Langley.

Freshspring raises steam on periodic weekends during the year and occasionally cruises in the Floating Harbour.

Tonnage: 283 gross, 93 net, 594 displacement.
Length: $126\frac{1}{4}$ft × beam $24\frac{1}{2}$ft. Water tanks capacity: 236 tons. Engines: Steam reciprocating triple expansion, 450ihp. Speed: $9\frac{1}{2}$ knots.

Yacht *Xenia* ex-*Aello* (Restored)

The auxiliary-powered schooner/yacht *Xenia*, lifted from the water and refitting on a quayside in Bristol City Docks, is currently (1987) revealing all her thoroughbred lines to the public. She was built as the *Aello* in Hamburg, Germany, to the designs of Max Oertz for a Greek owner, 1920–21. Her graceful wooden hull, clothing a steel frame, is fastened with yellow-metal bolts, and her lead keel weighs 32 tons. The planking of her weather deck is of selected wood covered with a layer of teak, and the deck fittings are of galvanised steel.

Below decks she was sumptuously fitted out. The German magazine *Die Yacht* of January 1921 says of her interior luxury: 'the floors are covered with soft, sound-proof carpeting, all the colour tones blend harmoniously, so that an interior of distinguished, peaceful elegance is created'.

Wilhelm Matolitz tailored her original sails from British-supplied material, and the full sail area of 416m^2 was made up as follows:

Mainsail	172·5m²
Schooner sail	76m²
Foresail	40m²
Jib sail	40·3m²
Large topsail	48·3m²
Fore topsail	20·5m²
Flysail	18·2m²

For manoeuvring in harbour a 50ps Lloyd engine was installed, driving a propeller whose blades could be disengaged by handwheel control on deck, to reduce 'drag' under sail.

Length: 29·5m (OA), 20·0m (waterline) × beam 6·0m. Draught 3·5m.

Schooner *Pascual Flores* (Afloat and at work)

'Whither, O splendid ship, thy white sails crowding,
Leaning across the bosom of the urgent west...'

So wrote Robert Bridges in 'A Passer-by', and all who share his sentiments will be cheered by the sight of the restored *Pascual Flores* under sail. Built in 1919 by Antonio Mari on the beach of Porrevivja, Spain, she was one of two sister ships; but what has become of her consort, the *Marguerita Flores* we have been unable to discover. The yard of their birth, however, is still in business, and still run by the same family.

Pascual Flores (English 'Easter Flowers') was designed as a deep-sea schooner for the transatlantic fruit trade, Spain to the USA. Fruit exporters had a preference for smaller vessels with shallower holds, as better suited for the conveyance of this crushable and perishable freight. A recent visitor to Spain met old-timers on the coast who remembered *Pascual Flores* with affection. They said she was nicknamed 'Cock of the Seas' and it would seem with good reason. She distinguished herself during a severe storm in the 'twenties when other vessels on her 'run' either put back or were given up for lost, 'but *Pascual Flores* came bucketing in on schedule with her cargo intact'. The same informant also learned on the Spanish coast that it was the custom to hold races every year for the fruit schooners, and that *Pascual Flores* invariably won the trophy whenever she was entered. During the 1930s a Spanish documentary film was made aboard her, and she was thereafter commonly known as the *Lady of Spain*.

In 1945 her sails and running rigging were removed and she was fitted with a Thornycroft engine. Thereafter for 10 years she worked as a motor salt-carrier on the Spanish coast. In 1955 she was extensively rebuilt and the Thornycroft engine was replaced by a two-cylinder two

Pascual Flores after her refit by Peter Gregson.

Pascual Flores in 1977, being reconditioned at Dartmouth.

stroke PEB of 100hp. Of her employment in the next few years we have no record, but she came into British ownership when Dartmouth schoolmaster Peter Gregson found her in Ibiza, and purchased her there.

We first saw *Pascual Flores* in July 1977, with one mast stepped, alongside Kingswear Quay. She was then in process of being re-rigged as a schooner for charter work, and a small squad of schoolboys were enthusiastically helping with odd jobs on deck. We saw her again, a year later, at moorings in the Dart, very smart, with painted ports, and almost ready for sea. Later she featured in the BBC TV series 'Kidnapped', from the RL Stevenson classic. In the autumn of '78 she was at Plymouth, where a 200hp Volvo engine was installed. Her canvas now consisted of fores'l, very large mains'l, triatic tos'l, gaff, inner and outer jibs, flying jib and main stays'l. Peter Gregson told us it was the intention to keep the ship under sail whenever possible, but she had to earn her living, and a powerful and reliable engine was necessary to enable her to meet requirements of modern business by being on schedule irrespective of wind and tide. He hoped that conferences, exhibitions and parties would prove a major source of income and to provide for these the ships main hold had been preserved as a large open space and was being fitted up for these purposes. The forehold had been partitioned and now comprised five double cabins, saloon, galley and bathroom, thus providing good accommodation for ten passengers. At this time the crew consisted of master, mate, engineer, bos'n, cook and deckhands (including two girls). The engineer was also a highly qualified diver, so diving instruction would be one of the special facilities the ship could provide. The future seemed hopeful, as *Pascual Flores* was also particularly suitable for film work: she had been authentically restored and was free of most of the anachronisms which make period filming difficult.

These dreams however were not to be fulfilled, and Peter Gregson sold *Pascual Flores* to the Nova Trust, who own the ship today, a registered charity based in Bristol. The intention of the Trust is to offer sail training and other educational opportunities in the *Pascual Flores* to disadvantaged young people. A comprehensive restoration is in hand under Project Shipwright Dave Green. This involves the vessel being re-masted with Douglas firs, and re-rigged as a tops'l schooner; while the hull has been subdivided by five new steel watertight compartments. The work is being carried out at Princes Wharf outside the lifeboat Museum; but when the ship is operational – it is hoped by the summer of 1988 – she will probably be moored in St Augustine's Reach.

Tonnage: 150 gross. Length: 133ft (OA) 96ft (on deck) × 28·0ft beam. Sail area: approx 4000 square feet.

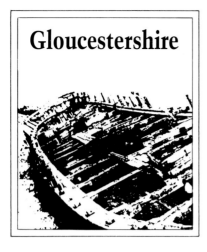

River Severn

Between Gloucester and Sharpness the Severn is no longer navigated as a commercial thoroughfare, and is often incorrectly described as unnavigable. But this is the realm of the famous Severn Bore; and if a bore is due, no stranger to the river should venture on it unaccompanied by a local river-man. In fact, all the hulks and ship-remains listed here are accessible by land.

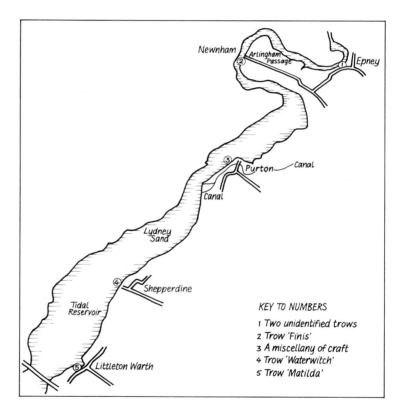

KEY TO NUMBERS

1 Two unidentified trows
2 Trow 'Finis'
3 A miscellany of craft
4 Trow 'Waterwitch'
5 Trow 'Matilda'

River Severn, East Bank

The Epney Hulks   ST 762111

In the mud of the river bank, just off the Anchor Inn, lie the remains of two trows, one 'decked' with concrete. All our efforts to identify them have failed.

Her name at last appropriate, the Finis *takes her last rest at Arlingham Passage.* Edwina Small.

Arlingham Passage

Trow *Finis* ST 695114

A double-ended trow built at Brimscombe, Stroud, in 1881 and registered at Gloucester. Her stern and rudder post are up against the bank, while her keel and floors support the broken remains of a World War II concrete pill box! Her last owner/skipper was Fred Wood, of Westbury-on-Severn.

Official number: 78707. Tonnage: 27 net.

The Purton Hulks

Those who enjoy hulk-hunting will certainly find Purton worth a visit. Here, north of Sharpness on the east bank of the Severn, and between the river and the Gloucester-Sharpness canal lie about 40 vessels in various stages of decay: some buried almost to the point of disappearance, others recognisable for what they were, a few with their identity known. All were run aground here to give their last service in an anti-erosion role, and all are readily accessible from the canal towpath, but the visitor is advised to don 'wellies'.

Some of the craft were never other than dumb towing barges, a few were under sail rig until the end, others were former seagoing ships cut down in their latter years for barge duties. The barges were towed on the canal by the long-departed steam tugs of the Sharpness New Docks and Gloucester and Birmingham Navigation Company of Gloucester. 'The tugs were of three categories', says Fred Rowbotham, former engineer to successive river authorities: 'the more seaworthy worked Sharpness to Avonmouth or Newport, the canal tugs Sharpness to Gloucester, and the river tugs Gloucester to Worcester and Stourport'. Well-remembered locally are the Bristol-built *Resolute* of 1896, and the Appledore-built *Primrose* of 1906. *Resolute* was a steel tug of 32hp and is still in existence, privately owned at Westbury on Severn: while *Primrose*, steel-built and 35hp, has also survived in private ownership, and according to Gloucester Library records, is actually at work – for British Waterways – in Yorkshire. On the Severn the barges were handled by the *Iris* of Bristol or the Lytham-built *Stonegarth* of 1910, or the *Victor*, which when converted from steam was renamed *Severn Victor*. All these tugs were indeed converted to diesel in their late working years to reduce operational costs.

Starting a tour of inspection from the northern end, the first hulk encountered is that of the Severn trow *Monarch*, now filled with soil and grassed over at deck level. Built

Her last duty a humble one, today
Monarch *reinforces the Severn
river bank, but in her day she was
the largest of her kind, and the
ultimate in trow construction.*
Edwina Small.

*Cows on the starboard beam! The
ketch* J. & A.R. *has forsaken the
maritime element for the rural.*
Edwina Small.

and registered at Saul in 1900 with the Official number 105409, the *Monarch* was owned by AS Rice of Gloucester. Described to us by Fred Rowbotham as 'a lovely vessel', the *Monarch* was one of half-a-dozen still-rigged trows in the 1920s, carrying grain from Avonmouth to Healing's Mill at Tewkesbury. Said to the largest Severn trow ever built, she was 80·8ft long and her tonnage figures were 93 gross and 76 net. The name 'Trow' is derived from the Anglo-Saxon word for trough, a reference to the typical large open hold of these vessels. The rig of the early trows was a single mast with a large square sail, but during the 19th century the tops'l ketch rig and plain fore-and-after in turn became popular. The *Monarch* was ketch-rigged.

On the *Monarch*'s starboard quarter is a cluster of five concrete barges, originally bearing the names *Sabrina I, II, III*, etc. These are some remaining examples of hundreds of their kind, built during World War II as a Government project for the storage and transport of grain, for which their capacity was 200 tons. They measure 100ft in length × 21ft beam and these at Purton worked between Avonmouth and Gloucester in the 'fifties. Just before the river bank is broken by a muddy inlet lie the remains of the ketch *J. & A. R.*, named with the initials of her erstwhile owners, the Rice brothers. Embedded deeply in the soil, she has broken open, the bow planking on the starb'd side having separated from the stem.

South of the inlet, and parallel to the river, lies the largest of the hulks. Retired mariner and ex-pilot George Reece informed us 'she was formerly a three-masted barque: I remember her afloat but I cannot recall her name'. Her main beam is missing, so we could not read her official number. Later enquiries however suggest that this is the three-masted tops'l schooner *Despatch*, whose figurehead has been preserved by Severn River shipwright Vic Gower of Saul. Immediately astern lie two more of the reinforced concrete *Sabrina* barges, and an anonymous vessel almost buried in the bank.

The larger of the next two hulks, which lie close together, is the *Severn Collier* (ex-*Severn*), a sloop-rigged freighter built at Bristol in 1858 with the Official number 21195. The name is still discernible on her transom stern, and her square iron rudder is still in position. Having a tonnage of 46, she was owned by the Severn & Canal Carrying Company Ltd of Gloucester, and spent her latter years conveying coal to Cadbury's chocolate factory via the Gloucester and Birmingham Navigation. Beyond her a stern post protrudes defiantly from the grass bank, indicating a vessel completely buried. Then comes quite a large wreck, surely a schooner, with the remains of her after bilge-pump still in place, and a maze of distorted iron rib-straps, and wrought iron knees supporting cracked beams confronting an intended archaeologist. Lying at right angles to this

Once a barquentine, later a schooner, and eventually cut down and named the 'King' her date and place of construction are a mystery. Edwina Small.

Europa, *the Sharpness dock's company's wrecking barge, is now very much a wreck herself.* Edwina Small.

Flower of the Severn, *the one-time Bristol-owned ketch in her last resting place at Purton.* Edwina Small.

anonymous schooner is a Severn Trow, the fastening-points for her side-cloths still visible.

Stern to the river, the next hulk is a former three-masted schooner cut down for barge work, in which capacity George Reece recalled she was popularly known as 'the King', though this was not her name when a seagoing ship. Frank Savage, retired captain of the tug *Primrose*, believes she was formerly named *Sally* and that her original rig was barquentine. Many of her beams are still in place, as are the fore and after bilge pumps, a massive samson post, and a number of 'tween deck air pipes. There is a great deal of forged ironwork in situ.

She had been brought to the Severn from Hull by Captain Walter Butt, and as the *River King*, was motorised and traded to Gloucester in the 1950s. Some yards further to the south is another ex-schooner, said to be either the *Shamrock* or the *Pioneer*, but our researches have failed to trace details of either.

With her bow in a very boggy area of the bank there lies, three vessels further on, the *Europa*. This was the old Dock Company's 'wrecking barge'. As such she had large bow sheaves, a boiler, donkey-engine and large winch for heavy lifting, and was used for working on ships which sank by mischance in the Severn fairway. The years of her prime as a seagoing schooner are veiled in mystery, for no one, it seems, can remember when she was *not* the Sharpness wrecking barge. We know however that her official number was 70430, that she was built and first registered at Middlesbrough in 1875, and that her net tonnage was 167. Today her lifting gear has all been removed, but the stalk of her after bilge-pump is still standing. Her port side has collapsed from midships to the sternpost.

Immediately south of *Europa* is another Severn trow, whose identity is uncertain, but probably the 69 tons Gloucester-registered *Abbey*, built 1900 and owned by GT Beard, Ltd. A nameless schooner lies between this trow and the *Flower of the Severn*. This romantically-named ketch, with an outside keel – unlike the trows – and two bilge keels, was built as a sloop at Lydney as early as 1841, and must surely be the doyen of the river bank. She had a net tonnage of 51, and at the turn of the century was owned by William Galbraith of Bristol. In spite of her age she is, excepting the concrete barges, the most complete hulk at Purton, with some of her upper deck intact, a portion of the deckhouse standing, and her rudder still on its pintles.

Two ships beyond lies the *Harriet*, a Severn flat of 33 tons, official number 69915, built and registered at Gloucester for local trading, in 1876. The flat, popular for estuary work in the 19th century, had a square stern with 'outdoor' rudder, flat bottom for taking the ground, mast in tabernacle for lowering, and a hold with about 60-ton capa-

Still graceful, the remains of the Gloucester flat Harriett *on the east bank of the Severn.*

Entirely filled with soil, the nondescript Huntley *lends her strength to the river bank at Purton.* Edwina Small.

city. (The well-known Mersey flats were rather larger). *Harriet*'s hull, which has tumblehome, is fairly well preserved. Her mast tabernacle and main pump are still in situ. Owned at the turn of the century by Jacob Rice & Sons Limited, of Gloucester, she was in the hands of Fred Ashmead of Bristol at the time of her withdrawal.

Nearby is the nondescript *Huntley* – her rig is not specified by the Mercantile Navy List. Official number 145627, she is a veritable youngster compared with some of her neighbours, having been built and registered at Gloucester in 1910.

A 51 tonner, her last owners were GT Beard, Ltd. A hundred yards further south lies the last of the hulks, a ketch reduced to barge, named the *Heart* and registered at Bristol. Among the unidentified wrecks are almost certainly the box trows *Dora* and *Sunbeam* and the Dutch barge *Twee Gususters*, all ketch rigged in their working days. The return walk can be made along the canal towpath. Here modern barges, which have usurped the work of our old friends, are often secured to the bank, and the diesel tug *Speedwell* may very likely be seen at work.

Shepperdine

Burnt Remains

On the foreshore just off the Windbound Inn at Shepperdine there lay until recent years the trows *Waterwitch* and *Onward*, abandoned there to support the sea wall. The *Waterwitch* was a built-upon trow, ie converted from an open-hold side-cloth trow to a 'box' trow with side decks and combings. Both hulks were set on fire and destroyed by local men in 1975 because the *Waterwitch* was damaging rather than protecting the bank when high tides were accompanied by westerly winds. Some derelict cars were put aboard to increase the conflagration. Fragments of burnt timber can still be seen on the bank.

Waterwitch Official number: 11656. 63 tons. Built: 1849 Stourport.
Onward Official number: 105407. 26 tons. Built: 1896 Brimscombe.

Littleton Warth

Trow *Matilda*   ST 588910

A pilgrimage to the remains of the *Matilda* may be disappointing. She lay in Littleton Pill until 1986 when shore development and pipe-laying caused her timbers to be broken out by mechanical diggers and dumped near the road at Whale Wharf.

The *Matilda* was built at Bridgwater in 1830 for a Newport merchant named John Young. She had several other owners before being bought in 1871 by George Wintle, a Littleton Brickworks owner. She thereafter worked from Littleton to Lydney with bricks, returning with coal, and periodically loaded sand for the brickworks from a midriver sandbank at New Passage. After Wintle's death his son sold the *Matilda* to the brothers Jim and Moses White who, it is thought, had actually worked the ship for the Wintles. On January 5 1885 a 68ft whale with a 12ft mouth was cast up beside *Matilda*'s berth at Littleton, and the brothers White arranged for two steam traction engines from Olveston to haul this prize above the tideline. Littleton became famous overnight. According to local tradition 40,000 people travelled from far and wide to see the monster before it was towed by water to Bristol to be cut down for manure. But the Brickworks, whose products reached their market via *Matilda* was renamed the Whale Brick, Tile Pottery Works, and even today a signpost points to Whale Wharf.

The death of Jim White during World War I left Moses White as master and sole owner for the rest of the ship's lifetime. He kept a spaniel on board named Billy 'which was always biting people'. The *Matilda* was damaged by resting on a pile in Littleton Pill *c* 1930 and was deregistered in 1932. Her binnacle is preserved by Olveston Historical Society, and her story, with that of Moses White is recorded in *Severnside Memories* by Christopher Jordan, published 1979.

Official number: 12928. Tonnage: 29 net. Length: 47·0ft × beam 14·0ft × depth 7·0ft.

Matilda, *before and after, in Littleton Pill.* NMM

The last vestiges of Matilda, *at Whale Wharf.*

Glossary of Nautical Terms

abaft, aftside behind (aboard, but nearer to the stern)

apron a timber behind the lower part of a ship's stem, performing a binding purpose.

backstays rope or wire stays from the topmast heads to the ship's sides (secured aftside the shrouds), to support the mast when the sails are drawing.

Baltic ketch Baltic Sea coasting vessel with ketch rig plus square sails on the mainmast.

barque a three-masted sailing vessel square rigged on fore and main, and fore-&-aft rigged on the mizzen. (There were some four-masted barques, square rigged on the mizzen, fore-&-aft on the jigger).

barquentine a three-masted vessel with the foremast square-rigged, and the main and mizzen fore-&-aft rigged.

beam **1** any sort of the transverse frames across a ship's hull supporting the main deck. The main beam bears the ship's official number. **2** the greatest width of a vessel.

bilge *n* the broadest part of a ship's bottom. *v* to spring a leak in the planking at the bilge.

boom a long spar reaching from the mast to extend the foot of a principal sail in fore-&-aft rig.

bow, bows forepart of a ship.

brigantine a two-masted vessel square-rigged on the foremast, and fore-&-aft rigged on the main. (The popular rig for British coasting vessels till the latter part of the last century).

bulkhead any of the vertical partitions separating the interior compartments of a ship.

bulwarks the sides of a ship above deck level.

bunker *n* compartment for holding coal fuel *v* to replenish with fuel.

chainplates iron plates bolted below the channels on the side of a sailing vessel, to which are attached the deadeyes holding the shrouds and backstays.

channels a wood or iron bracket projecting horizontally from a ship's side to spread the shrouds and hold them clear of the bulwarks.

dandy wink a small hand winch on the port side of some sailing trawlers for heaving up the after end of the trawl beam.

deadeye a round wooden block perforated with three holes for the lanyards which set up the shrouds and backstays: 'dead' in the sense of having no revolving sheave.

deadwood solid timbers bolted above the keel, for'rd and aft, to house the heels of frames which do not 'come down' to the keel.

depth in hold vertical measurement from keel to maindeck. One of the three 'vital statistics' of a ship.

displacement tonnage the quantity of water displaced by a ship afloat (variable according to load) and thus the actual weight of the vessel. The tonnage of warships is always reckoned in this way.

draught depth to which a ship sinks in the water when afloat: variable according to load.

fastenings bolts, pins or dowels securing the framework, and planking of a ship. Ships with iron fastenings designated accordingly in Lloyd's register. Ships with copper fastenings are popular with shipbreakers! Some small vessels were wood-dowelled.

Glossary of Nautical Terms

felted	indicates felt fitted to ship's bottom before sheathing.
floors	the lowest timbers in a ship's framing, between keel and futtocks.
forward	pronounced for'rd or for'ard, in or towards the front part of a ship.
forefoot	the junction of a ship's keel with the stem.
fore-&-aft rig	sails which are not set to yards.
foul bottom	**1** a ship's bottom when covered with barnacles, weed, etc. **2** the seabed if rocky or wreck-strewn.
freeboard	vertical measurement between water line and deck, variable according to load.
full and by	sailing close to the wind, but keeping everything full.
futtocks	shaped timbers rising from the floors to the frames.
gammon-knee	a shaped timber at the head of a ship's stem, projecting under the bowsprit.
garboard	the planks or plates of a ship's bottom nearest the keel.
gross tonnage	total cargo-carrying space of a ship, expressed in register tons, which equal 100 cubic feet. Does not signify the ship's actual weight.
gunwhale	pronounced gunnel. The wale or upper edge of a ship's bulwarks. (A ship's upper guns were pointed from it).
hatch	an opening in a ship's deck giving access to a hold or companion-way.
hawsepipe	a tubular casting in a ship's bows through which the anchor cable passes.
heave-to	to take the way off a ship and bring her to a virtual standstill.
hold	interior compartment of a ship, for stowage of cargo.
in ballast	without a cargo but with ballast (heavy material eg iron, stone or gravel low in the holds) for stability.
jib-boom	a spar run out from the bowsprit and extending the bowsprit forward. To it is lashed the tack of the triangular jib sail.
jury rig	temporary canvas rigged in an emergency eg loss of mast or sails.
keel	a ship's 'backbone'. The longitudinal member extending the length of the ship's bottom.
keelbolts	long bolts securing keel, floors and kelson.
keelson, kelson	the inner keel of a ship, binding the floor timbers to the keel proper.
ketch	small two-masted vessel having main and mizzen masts with fore-&-aft rig.
length (OA, BP, or WL)	various measurements of a ship's length. OA (overall) from stemhead to taffrail. BP (between perpendiculars at stem and sternpost). WL (waterline) ship's length on surface of the water.
lugger	a small vessel with one or two masts, whose rig is the lugsail – a fore-&-aft four-cornered sail set on a yard so that about one third of its length is before the mast.
mizzen-mast	the third mast in a three or four masted vessel, and the second mast in a ketch.
moulded depth	ship's vertical measurement from the keel to the fiferail ie depth in hold + height of bulwarks.
mule	a Brixham term for a class of sailing trawler with ketch rig like the larger 'sloops' but averaging only about 35 tons. Introduced in 1905.
net tonnage	gross tonnage less deducted spaces required for working the ship. The tonnage on which dues were calculated. Not a measure of weight. Some tugs had a net tonnage of nil.
paddlebox	the (approximately semi-circular) covering of a paddle-wheel to contain and deflect the turmoil of water.

paddle-sponson outward extension from a paddle-steamer's deck to accommodate the wheel and support the paddle-box.

pintles vertical pins on which a rudder is shipped and turns.

port the left side of a ship; superseded the earlier term 'larboard'.

portmark letters painted on bows of fishing vessels indicating their part of registry, and followed by the vessel's number.

pump windlass a windlass worked by iron levers which rock a crosshead in a pumping action as the windlass drum revolves. A type commonly fitted to coastal ketches.

reef, to to reduce the area of sail while leaving some of the sail set.

roller-reefing gear the general name for a number of patent devices for reefing large fore-&-aft sails by turning the boom and winding the foot of the sail around it.

rudder 'out of doors' a rudder which is entirely or almost entirely external ie the rudder does not pass thro' the hull, although its head may pass thro' the overhang of the counter.

salted vessel's hull timbers salted in accordance with Rules, Section 37 (wood ships).

schooner specifically, a fore-&-aft rigged sailing vessel of two masts, fore-&-main. Also, a similar vessel when carrying topsails on the foremast or similar vessels of three or more masts, if so designated (three-masted schooner).

shaft-tunnel the metal tube protecting the propeller-shaft between the engine and the sternpost.

shrouds a set of ropes or wires from masthead to ship's side, supporting the mast against lateral movement.

sloop a small single-masted cutter-rigged vessel with a fixed bowsprit; also a Brixham term for a ketch-rigged trawler of over 40 tons.

smack-rigged a small decked or part-decked sailing coaster or fishing vessel, rigged as a cutter, sloop or yawl.

spritsail, sprits'l four cornered, fore-&-aft sail spread from a diagonally placed boom (the sprit) as in a Thames barge.

starboard the right-hand side of a ship. Corruption of steerboard (*old English* steorbord) denoting side of ship where steering oar was shipped.

stem the foremost part of a ship's hull. In wooden vessels, the shaped timber in the bow to which the forward ends of the hull planking were fastened.

stemhead the topmost projection of a ship's stem.

sternpost the aftermost timber of a ship's frame, supporting the rudder. Many vessels had double or triple sternposts.

strakes a breadth of planking or plates in a ship, running from stem to stern.

tiller the bar or lever for turning a rudder.

tons burthen (or burden) a ship's carrying capacity expressed in tons, from the formula $\dfrac{\text{cubic feet} \times 74}{2{,}240}$.

top hamper any heavy encumbrance above a ship's upper deck; in distress circumstances, may include superstructure.

tops'l schooner a schooner with a topsail or topsail and t'gallantsail on the foremast.

tosher name given locally to Ramsgate sailing trawlers of just under 25 tons, built after 1894 to circumvent an act that year requiring larger trawlers to have certificated officers.

transom the timbers which in some vessels lie aftwart the sternpost and are bolted to the fashion timbers (the aftermost frames). Such vessels are said to have a square stern.

transon-rail	a shaped timber at the stern, between the taffrail and the deck.
windlass	a winch with a horizontal, controlled revolving drum sited on the foredeck, for hauling and hoisting, but especially for recovering the anchor.
yards	the spars on a mast which spread the square sails.
yawl	a variant of the ketch rig in small vessels, especially yachts. The mizzen is smaller in proportion and is shipped abaft the rudder post. The mizzen sheet is led to a bumpkin (light spar) extending from the stern.
yellow-metalled	indicates ship's hull has been sheathed with muntz (alloy of 60% copper, 40% zinc).

Bibliography

Barrow Wreck, The, Chris Jordan (Author 1978)
Cement, Mud and Muddies, Frank Wilmott
Colonial Clippers, The, Basil Lubbock (John Brown 1924)
Gaff Rig, John Leather (Adland Coles)
Golden Hind, The, Devon, (Lay Press Ltd Brixham)
Herald Express (files)
Inshore Craft of Britain, EJ March (David & Charles)
Lloyd's Register of Shipping
Mercantile Navy List
Merchant Schooners, The, Basil Greenhill (HMSO)
Newquay Owned Vessels between 1818 and 1976 GC White
Onedin Line, The, Alison McLeay (David & Charles)
Out of Appledore WJ Slade (Conway Maritime Press)

Portrait of Plymouth, JC Trewin (Robert Hale)
Potters' Field, The, LTC Rolt (David & Charles)
Sailing Trawlers, EJ March (David & Charles)
Sea Breezes (files)
Severnside Memories, Chris Jordan (Author 1979)
Ships Monthly (files)
Sprits'l, Richard Hugh Perks (Conway Maritime Press)
Western Morning News (files)
Westcotts and their Times, The (National Maritime Museum)
Westcountry Coasting Ketches, WJ Slade and Basil Greenhill (Conway Maritime)
Westcountry Harbour, Harold Trump (Brunswick Press)
Westcountry Passenger Steamers, Grahame Farr (T Stephenson & Sons)
Westcountry Sail, Michael Bouquet (David & Charles)

Index of Ship References

Index of Ship References